Other titles in the A Retreat With... *Series:*

A Retreat With Mother Teresa and Damien of Molokai

Caring for Those Who Suffer

Joan Guntzelman

ST. ANTHONY MESSENGER PRESS

Cincinnati, Ohio

Cover illustration by Steve Erspamer, S.M.
Cover and book design by Mary Alfieri
Electronic format and pagination by Sandy L. Digman

ISBN 0-86716-311-9

Published by St. Anthony Messenger Press
Printed in the U.S.A.

Contents

Introducing A Retreat With...

Twenty years ago I made a weekend retreat at a Franciscan house on the coast of New Hampshire. The retreat director's opening talk was as lively as a long-range weather forecast. He told us how completely God loves each one of us—without benefit of lively anecdotes or fresh insights.

As the friar rambled on, my inner critic kept up a *sotto voce* commentary: "I've heard all this before." "Wish he'd say something new that I could chew on." "That poor man really doesn't have much to say." Ever hungry for manna yet untasted, I devalued any experience of hearing the same old thing.

After a good night's sleep, I awoke feeling as peaceful as a traveler who has at last arrived safely home. I walked across the room toward the closet. On the way I passed the sink with its small framed mirror on the wall above. Something caught my eye like an unexpected presence. I turned, saw the reflection in the mirror and said aloud, "No wonder he loves me!"

This involuntary affirmation stunned me. What or whom had I seen in the mirror? When I looked again, it was "just me," an ordinary person with a lower-than-average reservoir of self-esteem. But I knew that in the initial vision I had seen God-in-me breaking through like a sudden sunrise.

At that moment I knew what it meant to be made in the divine image. I understood right down to my size eleven feet what it meant to be loved exactly as I was.

Only later did I connect this revelation with one granted to the Trappist monk-writer Thomas Merton. As he reports in *Conjectures of a Guilty Bystander*, while standing all unsuspecting on a street corner one day, he was overwhelmed by the "joy of being...a member of a race in which God Himself became incarnate.... There is no way of telling people that they are all walking around shining like the sun."

As an absentminded homemaker may leave a wedding ring on the kitchen windowsill, so I have often mislaid this precious conviction. But I have never forgotten that particular retreat. It persuaded me that the Spirit rushes in where it will. Not even a boring director or a judgmental retreatant can withstand the "violent wind" that "fills the entire house" where we dwell in expectation (see Acts 2:2).

So why deny ourselves any opportunity to come aside awhile and rest on holy ground? Why not withdraw from the daily web that keeps us muddled and wound? Wordsworth's complaint is ours as well: "The world is too much with us." There is no flu shot to protect us from infection by the skepticism of the media, the greed of commerce, the alienating influence of technology. We need retreats as the deer needs the running stream.

An Invitation

This book and its companions in the *A Retreat With...* series from St. Anthony Messenger Press are designed to meet that need. They are an invitation to choose as director some of the most powerful, appealing and wise mentors our faith tradition has to offer.

Our directors come from many countries, historical eras and schools of spirituality. At times they are teamed to sing in close harmony (for example, Francis de Sales, Jane de Chantal and Aelred of Rievaulx on spiritual friendship). Others are paired to kindle an illuminating fire from the friction of their differing views (such as Augustine of Hippo and Mary Magdalene on human sexuality). All have been chosen because, in their humanness and their holiness, they can help us grow in self-knowledge, discernment of God's will and maturity in the Spirit.

Inviting us into relationship with these saints and holy ones are inspired authors from today's world, women and men whose creative gifts open our windows to the Spirit's flow. As a motto for the authors of our series, we have borrowed the advice of Dom Frederick Dunne to the young Thomas Merton. Upon joining the Trappist monks, Merton wanted to sacrifice his writing activities lest they interfere with his contemplative vocation. Dom Frederick wisely advised, "Keep on writing books that make people love the spiritual life."

That is our motto. Our purpose is to foster (or strengthen) friendships between readers and retreat directors—friendships that feed the soul with wisdom, past and present. Like the scribe "trained for the kingdom of heaven," each author brings forth from his or her storeroom "what is new and what is old" (Matthew 13:52).

The Format

The pattern for each *A Retreat With...* remains the same; readers of one will be in familiar territory when they move on to the next. Each book is organized as a seven-session retreat that readers may adapt to their own schedules or to the needs of a group.

Day One begins with an anecdotal introduction called "Getting to Know Our Directors." Readers are given a telling glimpse of the guides with whom they will be sharing the retreat experience. A second section, "Placing Our Directors in Context," will enable retreatants to see the guides in their own historical, geographical, cultural and spiritual settings.

Having made the human link between seeker and guide, the authors go on to "Introducing Our Retreat Theme." This section clarifies how the guide(s) are especially suited to explore the theme and how the retreatant's spirituality can be nourished by it.

After an original "Opening Prayer" to breathe life into the day's reflection, the author, speaking with and through the mentor(s), will begin to spin out the theme. While focusing on the guide(s)' own words and experience, the author may also draw on Scripture, tradition, literature, art, music, psychology or contemporary events to illuminate the path.

Each day's session is followed by reflection questions designed to challenge, affirm and guide the reader in integrating the theme into daily life. A "Closing Prayer" brings the session full circle and provides a spark of inspiration for the reader to harbor until the next session.

Days Two through Six begin with "Coming Together in the Spirit" and follow a format similar to Day One. Day Seven weaves the entire retreat together, encourages a continuation of the mentoring relationship and concludes with "Deepening Your Acquaintance," an envoi to live the theme by God's grace, the director(s)' guidance and the retreatant's discernment. A closing section of Resources serves as a larder from which readers may draw enriching books, videos, cassettes and films.

We hope readers will experience at least one of those memorable "No wonder God loves me!" moments. And we hope that they will have "talked back" to the mentors, as good friends are wont to do.

A case in point: There was once a famous preacher who always drew a capacity crowd to the cathedral. Whenever he spoke, an eccentric old woman sat in the front pew directly beneath the pulpit. She took every opportunity to mumble complaints and contradictions—just loud enough for the preacher to catch the drift that he was not as wonderful as he was reputed to be. Others seated down front glowered at the woman and tried to shush her. But she went right on needling the preacher to her heart's content.

When the old woman died, the congregation was astounded at the depth and sincerity of the preacher's grief. Asked why he was so bereft, he responded, "Now who will help me to grow?"

All of our mentors in *A Retreat With...* are worthy guides. Yet none would seek retreatants who simply said, "Where you lead, I will follow. You're the expert." In truth, our directors provide only half the retreat's content. Readers themselves will generate the other half.

As general editor for the retreat series, I pray that readers will, by their questions, comments, doubts and decision-making, fertilize the seeds our mentors have planted.

And may the Spirit of God rush in to give the growth.

Gloria Hutchinson
Series Editor
Conversion of Saint Paul, 1995

Getting to Know Our Directors

Introducing Father Damien of Molokai

Under brilliant Hawaiian skies workmen climbed and crawled carefully, edging along the roof of the storm-damaged church. It was coming back into shape. Children scrambled on the ground near the base of the ladder, sifting through the dirt, picking up scraps of lumber and nails, sing-songing their own construction games. The back-and-forth scraping of a saw played a rhythm with the pounding nails and melody of voices.

"Bring those pieces closer together..."

"Hand me that hammer..."

"Move the ladder around to this side..."

The raspy voice of the foreman scratched the air, as he seemed to be everywhere on the roof, working side by side with the others. He was known for jobs like this. Time after time he'd be found in the middle of whatever needed to be done, never flinching from hard work, always joining in, at home in the group.

From the edge of the trees it looked like a common scene in any small village—everyone working together in time of need. A closer look produced a shocked double take. This was no ordinary work crew, no ordinary village. Some workers limped, fingers and toes were missing, skin was broken and sore, parts of bodies greatly deformed and crippled. The wreckage of the church paralleled the wreckage of the workers' bodies, even the foreman's. All were lepers—even the children on the ground. The foreman, too, suffered from leprosy contracted while living with the colony. His death was only months away. He was Father Damien, their priest.

Hard work on behalf of the lepers was the hallmark of his sixteen years with them. Intermingled with his priestly duties were jobs he'd never dreamed would be his. All the things he learned on his father's farm came to good use. When he faced the everyday needs of his motley community, where few seemed to have the resources or energy or interest in attending to them, Damien took them on, usually teaching himself. Many of the houses and shelters he built from scratch. Some he rebuilt along with his churches as they fell into disrepair. He learned to change dressings on wounds, to handle the administration of the leprosarium for a while and to dig graves. He planted and kept up with the weeding of his garden which fed the needy. Long and arduous treks were often necessary to be with someone suffering or in need. Nothing could stop him, no matter his weariness.

Now, his body weakening and deformed, and pain his constant companion, he still threw himself into strenuous physical work. He seemed to interpret all the needs of his lepers—like the damaged church roof—as letters with personal instructions from God sent directly to him. It was a trait that fueled and enabled him to care for his people through times of great loneliness and "black" thoughts and misunderstandings and the hardships of his chosen life. It also tended to provoke harsh and devastating criticism from some others, including his own religious superiors.

From his earliest days, determination and hard work were characteristic traits in Damien's life. Damien was his religious name. Strong and healthy from his birth in the little Belgian village called Tremeloo, he was named Joseph, the youngest son and seventh of the eight children of Frans and Anne-Catherine DeVeuster. Theirs was an ordinary Flemish family, dependable and devout, of average means, supported by Frans's farming and grain trading.

As in most farm families, the children learned the work early in life and grew into greater and greater responsibility, eventually able to relieve their elders. Yet, in the DeVeuster household the built-in workers found paths leading in other directions. Two children died early, Leonce and Gerard married, Eugenie and Pauline joined the Ursulines, and August became a priest. All hopes for carrying on the business fell on Joseph, apprenticed to his godfather in grain sales.

Off to school he went to learn French, the language of a good businessman in his part of the world. But as his body and knowledge grew stronger, so did a desire to do and be "more." He considered joining the Trappists but felt powerfully drawn to missionary work. So, despite the obstacles, Joseph's determination to follow what he read as God's invitation took over. That same determination that later carried him through the harshest of years eventually emerged in a youthful, somewhat dramatic and challenging letter to his parents. Threatening that to stop him from what he believed was his call from God "would be an ingratitude that would bring down cruel punishments"[1] on them, he asked to join his own brother August, now Brother Pamphile, in the Congregation of the Sacred Hearts of Jesus and Mary. Obviously aware that holding out for his last son to take over the business was a lost cause, young Joseph's father took him to visit his brother and wound up returning home alone.

In the Congregation Damien dove into whatever he saw God asking. He was more active than bookish. Because he showed little interest in being a scholar and his education lacked classical languages, he ran into his first obstacle in religious life: He was directed into the choir brothers. Because he so badly wanted to be a missionary priest, he immediately set to work to learn Latin, having already gained some everyday skill in French. No matter the amount of work involved, whatever he had to do to accomplish his goal he would do.

He was robust and strong, full of energy. Coming from a devout home he knew the lessons of self-discipline, and quickly incorporated these into his religious life. Pamphile, sharing a room with his brother, would awaken and find the other bed empty, Damien wrapped in a blanket sleeping on the floor. Pamphile remembered young Joseph choosing to sleep with a board under his mattress back in Tremeloo—a way of practicing self-discipline. In that same spirit, he would also see Damien holding back at mealtimes, leaving his share of the meat for others.

Brother Damien's determination transported him to the missions long before ordinary channels would have done so. At twenty-three he was still a student in minor orders when Pamphile, already ordained and twenty-six, prepared to leave for Hawaii—missionary country. Pamphile, however, developed typhus, rampant at that time in Louvain, and was dropped from the list of soon-to-depart missionaries. Damien, breaking all rules of protocol, boldly went over the heads of his own superiors, writing directly to the Superior General of the Order. He requested that he be allowed to go to Hawaii in Pamphile's place, even though he hadn't yet been ordained.

The priest-secretary to the Superior General suggested quick punishment for the rashness and impetuosity of this "misguided youth," lest others presume such privilege of dealing directly with their highest superior. With a kindly, wise and prophetic indulgence the Superior General responded, "The young man at Louvain should be, and will be, punished for his effrontery. To his Superior you will communicate the penalty for his transgression of discipline. He is sentenced to exile, banished to a life of servitude, loneliness and hard labor. In short, we will grant him the favor for which he so rashly pleaded. He may take his brother's place on the expedition."[2]

Two months after his arrival in Hawaii, Damien finished his studies for ordination and became a priest on May 21, 1864. In a letter to his brother he wrote that he felt his heart "would melt like wax, when for the first time I passed the bread of life to a hundred people there."[3]

Letters to his family reflected a never-ending joyousness and sense of privilege in being a missionary priest. In whatever he was doing—whether in difficulties or delights—Damien's almost childlike exuberance, energy and basic religious sense shone through. Even after painting a scene of great need and hardship, rigorous travel and sense of inadequacy, he finished one letter to his parents by saying, "Do not worry about me in the least, for when one serves God, one is happy anywhere."[4]

Puna, one of the six sections of the "big" island of Hawaii was Damien's first assignment, and his "parish" covered a huge area. In the course of eight months in Puna he'd become more fluent in the Kanaka language, built six "prayer houses," covered his territory (which took three days to cross) performing all the priestly duties of preaching, visiting the sick, assisting the dying and bringing the sacraments to far-flung locations. In a letter to the Superior General in his first year in the islands, Damien outlined his new life.

Instead of a tranquil and withdrawn life, it is a
question of getting used to traveling by land and by
sea, on horseback and on foot; instead of strictly
observing silence, it is necessary to learn to speak
several languages with all kinds of people; instead
of being directed you have to direct others; and the
hardest of all is to preserve, in the middle of a
thousand miseries and vexations, the spirit of
meditation and prayer.[5]

After these first eight months, Damien was asked to
transfer to Kohala, an area even more expansive than
Puna. A place "full of rocks, gorges and precipices,
innocent of roads and indeed even of paths in some
quarters, that district called for a robust man who could
handle a horse well and surmount all the obstacles in his
way."[6]

Early on Damien carried his "church" with him across
many miles and lush tropical growth, up and down cliffs,
across lava fields. As his weary horse plodded into a
populated area people scrambled to help him unload. The
warm and ready hospitality of the Hawaiian people
found a receptive, down-to-earth kindred spirit in this
new priest who would travel miles to find them. The slab
of wood he used for an altar and his sparse personal
belongings were just like him: simple and functional. He
lived as a poor man, once answering a question as to
where his house was by pointing to the saddle of his
horse and saying, "Here."

Gathered on the ground around one pot of food,
priest and family ate with their fingers and shared
whatever they had. Though Damien considered his
priesthood the highest of callings and he was strong in
his preaching to his parishioners—his children, as he saw
them—he always remembered he was an ordinary person
from an ordinary family.

In 1873 Damien sailed to a gathering of Sacred Heart Fathers on Maui for the blessing of a new church. While they were together, the bishop's conversation turned to the situation on the island of Molokai. With leprosy increasing and people's fear pushing for action, the government responded by creating a settlement on that sparsely populated island. The few Catholics on Molokai had no resident priest. The year before, a Sacred Heart brother had built a church there, Saint Philomena's, and several times a year a priest from Maui might manage a trip to Molokai for a day or two. But the whole island was very poorly served and needs were great, especially for those facing great suffering and death.

Bishop Maigret was reluctant to send any priest into such a situation of peril and loneliness. In their struggle about what to do, four priests offered to take turns at the leper colony, Kalawao, each one serving a designated time. Damien offered to be first to go. With the bishop's approval and his company on the ship, Damien sailed on the same ship that carried a contingent of lepers to Molokai. Little did he know that day that he was keeping an appointment with his destiny.

It did not take long for Damien to know he was home. Very quickly he wrote asking permission to remain—there would be no taking turns. Though several others came on occasion to work with him, Damien spent almost ten of his sixteen years on Molokai alone in his priestly duties, and would end his life in the service of "his lepers" a leper himself.

Despite the presumably good intentions of the government, Kalawao was a place of enormous suffering. Lepers of all ages were forcibly brought there after being "rounded up" and torn from their families and loved ones. Many felt like criminals being punished for something that they hadn't done, something over which they had no control. The island was steeped in sadness, grief and despair.

Feelings were mixed when word got out that a priest, a Father Damien, had come to stay. Some residents could not believe their good fortune. Others resented his intrusion into lives which had become promiscuous and wanton in their hopelessness and despair. Folks in and out of the colony expressed compliments and praise. Yet other missionaries, government workers, some residents and fellow priests voiced a variety of opinions and criticisms of his work. Damien was often puzzled that the very same action could call forth respect and admiration from some and harsh criticism from others.

Even in the outside world, when word traveled that a priest had gone to live at the leper colony, judgments varied. Some saw it as an act of heroism; others were sure it was a ploy for attention. Some resented Damien's invasion into the government's work there; others listened and learned from his suggestions. He quickly accomplished real improvements for the lepers—both through his hands-on care and attention, as well as suggestions for policy changes. But Damien heard others' opinions that he was seeking praise and notoriety.

Even his religious superiors came to interpret his determination (especially when he asked for supplies that were sorely needed by the lepers) as pushiness and manipulation. One wrote to the Superior General saying Damien "is a man almost completely wanting in judgment." And at a later time, "He needs a guardian; he is ineffective as a priest; he has no head; he is ill-mannered."[7] His new provincial superior wrote: "Damien is an overbearing man, capricious and proud. He had led people to regard him as the consoler and the nurse, etc., of the lepers; and he is nothing of the sort." In a letter of 1888, the year before Damien's death, this same superior wrote, "The worst of all our missionaries is Father Damien, who has been lifted so high by adulation that no one henceforth will succeed in getting him down to earth again."[8]

No matter what he did, it was deemed inappropriate— even when he developed leprosy. Damien's death itself failed to temper some of the harshness. A vindictive letter was published by a Protestant missionary who seemed to feel a great rivalry for Damien, calling the priest a "coarse, dirty man, headstrong and bigoted." In the letter he suggested Damien "caught" his leprosy by being inappropriately involved with leprous women.[9] Robert Louis Stevenson, having visited Father Damien and the leper colony, was incensed at such a vicious attack and wrote a strong letter of defense.

In the midst of such tribulations, which added to the burdens of his ordinary everyday life, Damien found great personal support and strength from his reception of the sacraments. Being an extremely conscientious, even somewhat scrupulous person, the opportunity for regular confession was most important to him. Despite his frequent requests, even pleading, for a confessor, he spent long stretches when no priest came and he was forbidden to leave. Once when government orders forbade lepers to board and non-leprous travelers to leave ship at Kalawao, Damien rowed out to the ship for confession. From his small boat, he confessed aloud in French to the priest on shipboard because the sacrament meant more to him than the embarrassment he experienced from such a lack of privacy.

Damien loved companionship. When visitors approached, even during his final months of suffering, he would be oceanside waiting as the small boat came from the ship, reaching out to steady the visitors as they stepped ashore, even helping with luggage. Near the end

of his life, after years of asking for sisters to come to help
with care of the lepers, a small group came to staff the
home for young girls. Damien was so excited he planned
a meal for the sisters. He could hardly wait for their
company and conversation. Yet they had been forbidden
by their superior to eat any food prepared by lepers, and
attempted to excuse themselves from the invitation.
Damien was crushed and pressured the sisters to eat with
him. Later he made the arduous journey to apologize for
his insistence to their superior—on his knees.

Damien worked until very close to his death. The
repair of the church was one of his last heavy jobs. Even
when his weakness forced him to remain on his straw
mattress he was thinking of the needs of his lepers. His
last written words were scrawled to the doctor, asking
him to see one of the lepers who was "spitting blood,"
remembering to give the doctor directions on how to find
the suffering man.

With all the understandable precautions meant to
prevent any other priest being infected by his leprosy,
Damien's great fear was that, after years of his own
loving care and ministry at the deaths of so many lepers,
he himself would have no priest to attend him. In the
end, several priests and other friends and helpers
surrounded him with their love and care. He was not
forgotten. He died on April 14, 1889 at the age of forty-
nine in the little house he had built near the cemetery on
Molokai.

Damien was not always easy to live with, or work
with. His biographer, Omer Englebert, describes him as
"brusque in speech, impetuous in temperament, and
careless in appearance."[10] It is tempting to say, as common
talk has it, that Damien "was no saint!" Yet on June 4,
1995, John Paul II beatified this farm boy, this plain and
simple, ordinary, unpretentious leper priest. This very

human man—not perfect, not polished, perhaps earthy and brusque—reached out with all he had, reached out to and saw God in those the world had shunned and judged of little value, and eventually "laid down his life for his friends."[11] This man can show us how close at hand God is, even in places the world refuses to look, in our own sickness and distress, and can minister to us with great love and real, practical devotion.

> Allow yourselves to be shaped by the Spirit! Holiness is not perfection according to human criteria; it is not reserved to a small number of exceptional beings. It is for everyone; it is the Lord who opens the way to holiness when we accept to collaborate, despite our sin and our at times rebellious temperament.... In your daily life, you are called upon to make choices which sometimes demand extraordinary sacrifices. This is the price of true happiness.[12]

Introducing Mother Teresa of Calcutta

It was close to Christmas and the Intensive Care nurse, working quickly and well to see to the care of her seriously ill patients, moved from one bed to the next to make her final assessment before change of shift. From the bed of their most noted patient who had again defied the odds—the exhausting effects of age and hard work and now the assault of heart surgery—came surprising directions: "Nurse, take all these tubes and things off of me. I feel like a Christmas tree!"

Mother Teresa was feeling better again and, with her sense of humor intact, was itching to return to her beloved poor and suffering in Calcutta and in the world. While she usually spoke with heartfelt seriousness and strong commitment in her loving attention to the sick and dying, the lepers and the ailing or abandoned children, her sense of humor would periodically break through, surprising and delighting those around her.

In fact, Mother Teresa was always her own person, startlingly independent, obedient, yet challenging some preconceived notions and expectations. She was strong in her opinions and profoundly determined. She was a stickler for traditional, conservative and self-disciplined Catholicism, prodding people (and, mostly, herself) to a clear and straightforward following of the Gospels and the hierarchy of the Church. Yet, her own life story includes many illustrations of her willingness to listen to and follow her own conscience, even when it seemed to contradict what was expected.

A notable example is the story of her "second calling" or "a call within my Vocation."[13] After fifteen years of vowed and dedicated life in the Sisters of Loreto, during which she taught young women from wealthy families in Calcutta, an inner voice spoke to her on a train ride to Darjeeling as she set off for her annual retreat. It was a call "to give up Loreto where I was very happy and to go out in the streets. I heard the call to give up all and follow Christ into the slums to serve him among the poorest of the poor."[14] So, despite the strong resistance of the Church to approving new communities, she set aside her commitment to the Sisters of Loreto to begin her own group, eventually gaining the Church's approval.

She was strong and authoritarian in her leadership, yet self-deprecating in her sincere statements of "I am not important." While respecting the priests of the Church, she resisted their "interference" with her community, in practice aligning herself with current feminist approaches to the patriarchal system, without ever calling her resistance by such a name.

Mother Teresa presented the same characteristic

stance toward the world, powerfully resisting the values of the times, very clearly following gospel values. Those our culture sees as of little or no value—the poor, the sick (especially those with diseases seen as "deserved" or "self-inflicted," like AIDS), those with unwanted pregnancies, the dying who remind us of our own relentlessly approaching deaths—she literally and tenderly embraced.

This strong and independent Slavic woman was born Gonxha (Agnes) Bojaxhiu in Skopje, Yugoslavia, on August 27, 1910. Five children were born to Nikola and Dronda Bojaxhiu, yet only three survived. Gonxha was the youngest, with an older sister, Aga, and brother, Lazar. This brother describes the family's early years as "well-off," not the life of peasants reported inaccurately by some. "We lacked for nothing."[15] In fact, the family lived in one of the two houses they owned.

Nikola was a contractor, working with a partner in a successful construction business. He was also heavily involved in the politics of the day. Lazar tells of his father's rather sudden and shocking death, which may have been due to poisoning because of his political involvement. With this event, life changed overnight as their mother assumed total responsibility for the family, Aga, only 14, Lazar, 9, and Gonxha, 7.

Lazar remembers the strength of their mother. "What would have become of us without my mother, I don't know. I feel that we owe her everything."[16] This shrinking family that once lived a comfortable life, now had little. Yet their mother "worked wonders"[17] as Lazar remembers, keeping them all together in their family home and finding ways to support them.

Before Nikola's death, their home had been a real center of political discussion and interest, always full of visitors and friends. But afterward, Dronda's intense religious interest and commitment prevailed. The family had always been God-fearing and concerned about others and, now under their mother's direction, their religious belief and expression intensified. "We were very disciplined Catholics in our house," Lazar remembers. "That same discipline is the backbone of Mother Teresa's order."[18] The family members helped organize church activities, sang in the choir, participated in church meetings, and cared for those in need. Lazar remembers a woman of their town whose family refused to see to her needs when she developed a tumor. His own mother brought her home and took care of her until she no longer was in need.

Though so much of her young life was centered in the Church, Mother Teresa later revealed that until she reached eighteen, she had never thought of being a nun. During her early years, however, she was fascinated with stories of missionary life and service. She could locate any number of missions on the map, and tell others of the service being given in each place.

At eighteen, Gonxha decided to follow the path that seems to have been unconsciously unfolding throughout her life. Taking her cues from both her parish priest—a Jesuit whose order was founded by the soldier Saint Ignatius—and her own experience of religious discipline, Gonxha chose the Loreto Sisters of Dublin, missionaries and educators. This group of sisters, founded in the seventeenth century to educate young girls, based their rules on those of this same Saint Ignatius.

In 1928, the future Mother Teresa began her religious life in Ireland, far from her family and the life she'd known, never seeing her mother again in this life, speaking a language few understood. During this period a sister novice remembered her as "very small, quiet and shy," and another member of the congregation described her as "ordinary."[19] Mother Teresa herself, even with the later decision to begin her own community of religious, continued to value her beginnings with the Loreto sisters and to maintain close ties. Unwavering commitment and self-discipline, always a part of her life and reinforced in her association with the Loreto sisters, seemed to stay with her throughout her life.

One year later, in 1929, Gonxha was sent to Darjeeling, to the novitiate of the Sisters of Loreto. In 1931, she made her first vows there, choosing the name of Teresa, honoring both saints of the same name, Teresa of Avila and Therese of Lisieux. In keeping with the usual procedures of the congregation and her deepest desires, it was time for the new Sister Teresa to begin her years of service to God's people. She was sent to Saint Mary's, a high school for girls in Entally, a district of Calcutta. Here she began a career teaching history and geography, which she reportedly did with dedication and enjoyment for the next fifteen years. It was in the protected environment of this school for the daughters of the wealthy, with its huge walls enclosing comfort, and even opulence, so greatly in contrast with its poor and squalid surroundings and people, that Teresa's new "vocation" developed and grew. This was the clear message, the invitation to her "second calling," that Teresa heard on that fateful day in 1946 when she traveled to Darjeeling for retreat.

During the next two years, Teresa pursued every avenue to follow what she "never doubted" was the direction God was pointing her. She was "to give up even Loreto where I was very happy and to go out in the streets. I heard the call to give up all and follow Christ into the slums to serve him among the poorest of the poor."[20]

Technicalities and practicalities abounded. She had to be released formally, not from her perpetual vows, but from living within the convents of the Sisters of Loreto. She had to confront the Church's resistance to forming new religious communities, and receive permission from the Archbishop of Calcutta to serve the poor openly on the streets. She had to figure out how to live and work on the streets, without the safety and comfort of the convent. As for clothing, Teresa decided she would set aside the habit she had worn during her years as a Loreto sister and wear the ordinary dress of an Indian woman: a plain white sari and sandals.

The security and camaraderie of community life was gone. Teresa was thrown back upon herself and God, and her belief in her call. "Leaving Loreto was for me the greatest sacrifice, the most difficult thing I have ever done. It was a lot more difficult than leaving my family and country to become a nun. Loreto was everything to me."[21]

Teresa first went to Patna for a few months to prepare for her future work by taking a nursing course with a group of American missionary sisters. In 1948 she received permission from Pius XII to leave her community and live as an independent nun. So back to Calcutta she went and found a small hovel to rent to begin her new undertaking.

Wisely, she thought to start by teaching the children of the slums, an endeavor she knew well. Though she had no proper equipment, she made use of what was available—writing in the dirt. She strove to make the children of the poor literate, to teach them basic hygiene. As they grew to know her, she gradually began visiting the poor and ill in their families and others all crowded together in the surrounding squalid shacks, inquiring about their needs.

Teresa found a never-ending stream of human needs in the poor she met, and frequently was exhausted.

Despite the weariness of her days she never omitted her prayer, finding it the source of support, strength and blessing for all her ministry. She would pray often with the Little Sisters of the Poor, a congregation of kindred spirits who also cared for the indigent and suffering. Gradually opportunities for assistance and support from others began to emerge.

Teresa was not alone for long. Within a year, she found more help than she anticipated. Many seemed to have been waiting for her example to open their own floodgates of charity and compassion. Young women came to volunteer their services and later became the core of her Missionaries of Charity. Others offered food, clothing, the use of buildings, medical supplies and money. As support and assistance mushroomed, more and more services became possible to huge numbers of suffering people.

From their birth in Calcutta, nourished by the faith, compassion and commitment of Mother Teresa, the Missionaries of Charity have grown like the mustard seed of the Scriptures. New vocations continue to come from all parts of the world, serving those in great need wherever they are found. Homes for the dying, refuges for the care and teaching of orphans and abandoned children, treatment centers and hospitals for those suffering from leprosy, centers and refuges for alcoholics, the aged and street people— the list is endless. In response to a request from Paul VI to open a house in Rome, Mother Teresa went to determine what the needs might be. After a tour through the city, seeing the wretched conditions of so many people, she returned to the Pope and said, "Your Holiness, God seems to have left work for us to do just about everywhere."[22] And so her missionaries have gone just about everywhere.

Mother Teresa's work and followers have taken on

many forms, offering a host of opportunities for those who desire some association. Her Missionaries of Charity, the earliest community of those working closely with her, continues to grow with membership and service around the world. She began the Missionary Brothers of Charity in 1963. Mother Teresa has called another collection of coworkers her "second self."[23] In fact, this group, called the International Association of Co-Workers of Mother Teresa, was founded in 1969 and aggregated to the Missionaries of Charity. These she divides into three groups. The simple coworkers help through prayer, collecting supplies and resources, fund-raising, sometimes finding practical ways to help the poor in their own neighborhoods, putting a great deal of love into all their tasks. The second group is her sick and suffering collaborators who associate themselves and their sufferings with the work of the order and agree "to love and serve Jesus, not by what they offer, but by what they take."[24] The third group are those in the contemplative houses, called Missionary Sisters (or Brothers) of the Word. Mother Teresa saw these houses as wellsprings of intensive prayer to be the support of all the service offered by her workers.

Until her death in 1997, Mother Teresa continued her work among the poorest of the poor, depending on God for all of her needs. Honors too numerous to mention had come her way throughout the years, as the world stood astounded by her care for those usually deemed of little value. Among the many accolades she received was the Nobel Peace Prize in 1979, giving her the opportunity to speak to the world in the name of her beloved poor. Though she resisted personal attention, she was never unwilling to be acknowledged when she could bring attention to the needs of the poor. In her own eyes she was "God's pencil—a tiny bit of pencil with which he writes what he likes."[25]

Despite years of strenuous physical, emotional and spiritual work, Mother Teresa seemed unstoppable. Though frail and bent, with numerous ailments, she always returned to her work, to those who received her compassionate care for more than fifty years. Only months before her death, when she became too weak to manage the administrative work, she relinquished the position of head of her Missionaries of Charity. She knew the work would go on. Finally, on September 5, 1997, after finishing her dinner and prayers, her weakened heart gave her back to the God who was the very center of her life.

> I give fervent thanks to God who gave this woman of unshakable faith as a gift to the Church and to the world in order to remind us all of the supremacy of evangelical love, especially when it is expressed in humble service of the least of our brothers and sisters. I am confident that the memory of Mother Teresa's extraordinary spiritual vision, her attentive and self-sacrificing love of Jesus in each individual, her absolute respect for the value of every human life and her courage in facing so many challenges will inspire her spiritual daughters and sons to carry on her mission through their religious consecration and in cheerful, wholehearted care of the poorest of the poor.[26]

Placing Our Directors in Context

Though they lived many years apart, Damien's world of the mid-nineteenth century had much in common with Teresa's, which covered almost the whole of the twentieth. In fact, though the times were different and their service at opposite ends of the world, these two lived as though cut from the same cloth and following the same pattern.

Despite the external life, values and possibilities the world held out, both seemed to exist within a different reality, a world more real and important than what they found all around them. In this more real world, they spent themselves lavishly caring for the poorest of the poor, whose poverty took many forms. Both Teresa and Damien, while utterly committed to their own Catholic beliefs, transcended boundaries of religion and life-styles and gave loving care to anyone in need. For them, everyone they saw was God in disguise.

We know Teresa's environment because it is our own, but we will find her a sister to Damien in spirit and service. The same human suffering that provided the context of their worlds continues to exist. The homeless, those with AIDS, cancer and other fearsome diseases (lepers of our own day), the unwanted and the dying are still ignored. Pain, suffering and poverty may be our own crosses. Damien and Teresa can speak to us today, nurture us and be our mentors in our struggle within our world and ourselves.

Damien's World

Damien could have lived at any time in the world's history and probably would have been just as unaffected by what was happening all around him. Born just before the middle of the nineteenth century, Damien lived during a time of great change. Cities were growing and commercial enterprises burgeoning. Though Damien's life took him into some of the bigger, bustling centers of his world, he seemed untouched by the excitement many found there.

The Belgium of Damien's youth was, as now, divided north and south into two culturally distinct areas. In the northern part of the country lived the Flemish—Damien's family and forebears; and in the south lived the Walloons, with their French language and culture. In *Damien: Hero of Molokai* Englebert notes that the Flemish people "brought honor to Christian civilization and to humanity."[27] They were rugged, hardworking, intelligent folks who were versatile and adaptable. Quite devout, the vast majority were Catholic, every village marked by its church. Their families were large with numerous vocations to religious life. A higher than ordinary percentage of these religious became missionaries.

So while the industrial revolution was afoot, while the preliminaries to civil war were rumbling in the United States, and metropolitan centers were growing and attracting workers from their surrounding rural areas, Damien remained somewhat heedless of all this activity, single-mindedly focused on the call he felt so strongly. This call would take him half a world away to a tiny island in the South Seas.

The islands of Hawaii in the nineteenth century were struggling with the intrusion of the outside world, especially illnesses introduced by foreigners. Inhabited by Polynesian people for centuries, the earliest known European visitor was the British explorer Captain James Cook with his company in 1778, less than one hundred years before Damien's arrival. Living in such total isolation, the islanders had no natural immunity to European diseases. Within a century of Cook's arrival, more than ninety percent of the population had died from newly introduced illnesses.

Leprosy threatened to destroy the Hawaiian population, in spirit as well as in body. As the presence of the disease became increasingly common, fear developed and grew. Those infected were rounded up and sent to the leper settlement of Kalawao, which had been established in 1865. Victims of leprosy were still treated like the lepers of Old Testament times. Men, women and children were seen as unclean, judged as having somehow brought the disease on themselves. In the absence of real scientific knowledge of its origins, the common belief tied leprosy to heredity or to syphilis, a sexually transmitted disease. Not unlike sufferers of AIDS today, victims were often judged, avoided and seen as somehow deserving their affliction. Families were expected to report and "turn in" relatives when the disease became apparent. Refusing the pain of separation, some healthy people accompanied their loved ones to the settlement, living out their lives there.

Kalawao, on one of the most remote peninsulas of Molokai, was accessible only by boat. Before Damien's arrival, little government assistance was available. Those sent to what they saw as their last dwelling on earth were expected to live out a wishful fantasy of the authorities and develop a self-supporting community, in which they were to farm and care for each other. They were to be isolated and self-sufficient. In actuality, the grief, depression, despair, isolation, physical pain and suffering, feelings of abandonment and hopelessness of the inhabitants created just the reverse. When Damien arrived he found a sinkhole of suffering. Lawlessness, promiscuity, poverty, pain and misery prevailed.

Within the chaos Damien, with his genuine religious spirit and concern for souls, gradually developed a more humane and spiritual setting for what became his community. He started from scratch. Just as there were no homes or dwellings for the lepers who arrived, there was none for him. He slept under a pandanus tree, ate his meals and lived in the open, near St. Philomena's Church. Finally, some lumber arrived from Honolulu and, as he would do for many others in the future, he built his own

small house. Throughout his days with the lepers,
Damien was forever working to make life more bearable,
more livable and more humane for his people. He became
the instigator, the developer and the creator of whatever
he found was missing, whether physical, emotional, or
spiritual.

Damien's world was always the one he found at
hand, the one he lived in with those he served. He threw
himself wholeheartedly into his commitment to God,
often doubting himself and his own worthiness, but never
doubting the needs of his charges. That didn't insure that
others would see him or the lepers in the same way.
Admired and respected by some, he often lived in conflict
with both government and religious superiors, as well as
with Protestant missionaries who resented his presence.

Teresa's World

Mother Teresa's life took long strides across most of
the twentieth century. From her early experiences of
horse-drawn carriages, to boats, to automobiles, to trains
and planes, she witnessed humans on the moon, living on
space stations and probing Mars. Technology developed
at an amazing rate and played the major role in nearly
every aspect of human life.

Her young days were spent in the village of Skopje, a
provincial capital of the area, at that time part of
Macedonia, which later became Yugoslavian territory.
Now a city of four hundred thousand, during Teresa's
youth Skopje's population was closer to twenty thousand.
It was a town that in some ways prefigured what the
whole world would come to be, where mixed
nationalities and religions lived side by side. The whole
Balkan territory was unstable as the Ottoman Empire
weakened and experienced a number of uprisings during
the century. Teresa lived in a part of the world that served

as a crossroads.

Her family had been Catholic for generations, devoted to their Church and its beliefs and activities, surrounded by others of a variety of faiths. Perhaps this experience laid the groundwork for her later openness and acceptance of people of other beliefs and religious orientation. With her father's interest and involvement in politics, Teresa understood how politics could help or hinder the people it was meant to serve. She would contend with this in both the religious and governmental systems of her missionaries' work.

By the time Teresa had decided to leave home and enter a religious community, she was already experienced in some of the circumstances she would find later in life. She became a citizen of the world. Starting with her inauguration into religious life in Ireland, where she learned English and the rigorous life of the Sisters of Loreto, this simple Albanian woman eventually covered the globe. While the particulars differed, in every country she visited Teresa experienced the upheaval and struggle of the people for justice and a decent life. Others were struggling for domination.

Not long before her arrival in Ireland, Irish nationalists led a rebellion against England and were severely crushed. Then she went on to India, where the political and social situation was somewhat confused. India only received its independence in 1947. For the two years of her novitiate, until she made her religious vows, Teresa lived in the beauty of Darjeeling, a resort area for wealthier Indian families, at the foot of the Himalayas and close to the jungle. From here she was sent to Calcutta to teach the daughters of wealthy families.

It was in Calcutta that she began to witness the terrible poverty and suffering of the poor and the great disparity that existed between those she taught and the poor outside her window. Calcutta had been long known as "the cesspool of the world,"[28] and its streets eventually became Teresa's home. Even the archbishop of the area was skeptical about Teresa's request to leave her beloved Loreto convent and begin her own service to the poorest of the poor. Not many of those she knew saw her choices in a favorable light. After hearing a "call" to care for the poor, Calcutta is where she began her new ministry outside the protection of convent walls.

Teresa lived immersed in this world where the needs of a large portion of humanity were simply ignored. Though most of her work was in India, she eventually traveled throughout the world and found poverty everywhere. Those who enjoyed riches and property seemed to resent the presence of the have-nots, as though these others did not, or should not, exist. These poorest of the poor became Teresa's everyday companions. To her, each person she encountered or cared for was Jesus living in the streets and asking for her attention and care.

While she spent most of her life in Calcutta, her notoriety grew. She applied for and received Indian citizenship, which she maintained until her death. Others with hearts open to the needs of the poor came to join her. Eventually Teresa was known around the world, and those wanting to share in her ministry were organized into the Missionaries of Charity and related groups.

In some places, Mother Teresa was criticized. These criticisms centered around her inclination to hold fast to her own beliefs and give little, if any, attention to root causes of the world's problems. The Second Vatican Council, the First and Second World Wars, the Korean and Vietnam Wars played out around the world, without distracting Mother Teresa. Some felt she avoided or simply ignored addressing the causes of poverty. She also held fast to her rejection of birth control in one of the world's most overcrowded areas.

While she rejected or ignored much that the world around her offered, she did choose to participate in the latest in medical care, even accepting the implantation of a pacemaker in her heart. She also willingly traveled by airplane when circumstances called for it.

Like Damien, her world tended to be one that was much narrower than the bigger world around her. Her eyes were set on the task at hand as she saw it, and that task received her entire attention.

Notes

[1] Damien to Parents, December 25, 1858, quoted in Gavan Daws, *Holy Man: Father Damien of Molokai* (New York: Harper & Row, 1973), p. 22.

[2] John Farrow, *Damien the Leper* (New York: Image/Doubleday, 1954), pp. 11-12.

[3] Omer Englebert, *Damien: Hero of Molokai* (Boston: St. Paul Books & Media, 1994), p. 52.

[4] Daws, p. 35.

[5] Daws, p. 38.

[6] Englebert, p. 59.

[7] Englebert, p. 206.

[8] Englebert, p. 207.

[9] Daws, p. 14.

[10] Englebert, p. 191.

[11] John 15:13.

[12] Beatification Ceremony, John Paul II, 1995.

[13] Robert Serrou, *Teresa of Calcutta: A Pictorial Biography* (New York: McGraw Hill, 1980), p. 38.

[14] Serrou, p. 38.

[15] Serrou, p. 25.

[16] Serrou, p. 25.

[17] Serrou, p. 25.

[18] Serrou, p. 26.

[19] Serrou, p. 31.

[20] Serrou, p. 38.

[21] Serrou, p. 40.

[22] Lush Gjergji, *Mother Teresa—Her Life, Her Works* (Hyde Park, N.Y.: New City Press, 1991), p. 86.

[23] Gjergji, p. 109.

[24] Gjergji, p. 115.

[25] *National Catholic Reporter*, September 19, 1997.

[26] Telegram of Pope John Paul II to Sister Nirmala Joshi, Missionaries of Charity Superior (*Crux of the News*, Gabriel Publishing Co., Latham NY, September 15, 1997).

[27] Englebert, p. 11.

[28] Serrou, p. 32.

DAY ONE

Seeing Clearly

Introducing Our Retreat Theme

"I haven't got time for the pain...," the lilting voice croons across the airwaves, voicing the fantasy that somehow our busyness can fend off the unwelcome truth of our lives.

How our world wants such a dream to be real—not only when we suffer ourselves, but also when we look on at the misery of so many others. Yet along with its abundance of blessings, life periodically flips to the other side of the coin and presents to each of us, whether we "have time" for it or not, suffering, sorrow, pain and distress.

Whether at any given moment we are the sufferers or the caregivers, we must battle what our everyday world teaches—that those suffering "brought it on themselves," or "it's God's punishment for their sins," or "forget them and look out for number one." It takes effort to wrench ourselves from the way our society sees and judges. "My thoughts are not your thoughts," God says in the Bible, "and your ways are not my ways."[1] As a matter of fact, in the very places we shun as repulsive or fearsome, God is disguised and waiting.

Mother Teresa and Father Damien refused to look the other way, refused to pretend. They chose to walk head-on into all that we want to avoid, the most extreme

suffering and death that continue to be part of life.
Though their human sensibilities couldn't help but suffer
assault, no fear, repulsion or pretense of the world
stopped them from finding God in the most afflicted and
shunned. And finding God there meant they found fertile
ground for their own becoming and growth in holiness.
Eventually they even came to know firsthand that other
side—the side of the afflicted one—both living their own
personal suffering in body and in spirit.

Choosing them for our mentors for this retreat means
choosing to walk into places that will threaten and assault
us. It means pushing ourselves to wake up to their ways
of seeing, even when everything in us is shouting for us
to look the other way. It means allowing them to love us
and care for us in our own suffering and need, and to
guide us in our care of others. Accompanying Teresa and
Damien also means walking into a battle, not only with
our world, but with ourselves. They will shake us out of
our comfort and dare us to face how different are God's
thoughts and ways from our own. They challenge us to
find God "in his most distressing disguise,"[2] whether
within ourselves or in others, knowing that if we do not
find God there we may never find God.

Opening Prayer

Damien and Teresa, kindred spirits,
I hesitantly come to be with you, though I'm afraid of
  the closeness.
I'm afraid of what you might ask of me, not sure that
  I can handle it.
I want your help, your wisdom, and yet I feel you are
  so far beyond me.
Perhaps we can begin gently.

You both were often so gentle with those you tended.
See all my needs and broken places.
Yet also see my desire to open up to God's work in me.
Perhaps we can begin by you showing me what you
　see.
Open my eyes to see the way God sees.
Show me how to change my way of thinking
So all my suffering and the suffering of others
Can lead me to find God's hiding places,
Even when they are heavily disguised.

RETREAT SESSION ONE

[H]e had no form or majesty that
we should look upon him,
nothing in his appearance, that
we should desire him.
He was despised and rejected by others;
a man of suffering and
acquainted with infirmity;
and as one from whom others
hide their faces...[3]

Right before our eyes looms a figure that could have
walked out of this Scripture. A man in shabby black robes
appears, looking decrepit and tired. Despite efforts to
hide it, traces of pain are etched across his face as he
shuffles into our meeting room. An involuntary gasp
pierces the air as the group draws back at the sight of
him. As one, we look away from his puffy, lumpish and
reddened face, small glasses perched on his misshapen
nose. Feeling a pull to glance back we notice his hands,
swollen, red, with broken skin alongside the calluses of
hard work. Somehow we know from his emaciated look,

his pain and the whole vulnerable feel of his presence that he is not far from death.

Holding his weight with his poor hands on the chair's armrests he eases his body down to sit in our circle, and we wince at his pain. But as he settles into his chair he sighs and a smile replaces the look of pain, gradually illuminating his face. This is Father Damien, the leper priest of Molokai. Despite his afflictions he loves gatherings like this. For so many years he craved companionship in his spiritual journey and rarely found it. Now he delights in the opportunity, and wants to be here even more than we do.

So captivated and repelled are we by the look of him we hardly notice the small, plain woman in a white blue-edged sari, rough sandals on her feet, who darts in and takes a seat next to him. She's almost twice his age, yet moves with a quickness and purpose that belie her long years and failing health. She clasps her gnarled hands in her lap and with her bright eyes smiles a greeting to all of us, conveying somehow that she has no time to waste. She turns to the pitiable man at her side and leans toward him in greeting. "I've wanted to meet you for a long time," we hear Mother Teresa say to Father Damien, reaching out her hand with no hesitation or sign of repugnance. He smiles again and clasps her hand, and we know we're in the company of loving kindred spirits.

The low whispers of conversation that had fallen on the group fade to an expectant hush that rolls like a wave across the bright room. We watch their faces closely for some sign of resistance as they take in the motley group of participants. But only love shines from the eyes of Teresa and Damien as they see our worried faces, wasting bodies, the eagerness for acceptance, the need for love and understanding, the fear and sadness in the circle around them. They seem perfectly at home. They know from experience that in just such people as us God hides and they choose this place. Ours is a group full of pain, suffering, human illness, distress and need. Several are outcasts—homeless and poor, some have a dreaded cancer diagnosis, some AIDS, one is soon to die. Another few want to learn how to serve and care for those suffering. We are all eager to be seen and heard but fearful from past experience that we will not be. So many people avoid us. But then, we would probably avoid our situations, too, if only we could.

"What a blessing for us to be together today!" Mother Teresa begins as she looks around the room. Father Damien smiles and nods.

Questions bump together in our minds. We hunger for them to make sense of this world and all its misery, to help us make sense of our own lives, our own suffering. We want to know how on earth they care for people with such horrible conditions, touch them, hold them, look at them, even love them. Aren't they put off by the smells and rags and dirtiness of it all? Aren't they afraid they will catch something awful? Look at Damien! How can he smile now, knowing he had been so healthy and strong and could do so much before his leprosy? How in the world can they find God in such terrible situations? Can they find God in us? Don't they see that sick and poor people probably have a lot to do with their own conditions? Probably brought a lot of it on themselves? Aren't we somehow, suffering people, responsible for ourselves? We've certainly heard all that from others and even say such things to ourselves sometimes.

"Jesus insisted," Mother Teresa's voice is clear, "that we love one another as he loves each one of us."[4] What a good way to begin our time together, knowing we all live and move in that great love, no matter how needy or poor or sick we are, that it surrounds us and that we can share it with each other."

It is no surprise that she began with the words of Jesus. Someone once said that she is "obsessed with the gospel." And through the morning we begin to discover what fuels her and Father Damien, what is the very root of their lives. They take the gospel seriously. They read it and live it as though it is true!

Both Teresa and Damien have a way of looking that sees through the surface of life to the realities hidden within. They want to be sure the words of Scripture aren't true of them when God says, "My ways are not your ways, nor my thoughts your thoughts." Both of them live by a vision, a singleness of seeing, that plays out in their lives and focuses them on God's thoughts and God's ways. No one could do such work, it seems, without that ability to see differently than the world sees, to be able to see with a clarity unknown to most.

Their vision—the foundation upon which they have built their lives—while clear as mountain air for them, is often puzzling to a world that tends to live on the surface, to not look beyond the surface. "We must begin talking about 'eyesight' today, about vision," Mother Teresa begins, "but not the way you may be thinking about it. We get so lost when we think that what we see on the surface is everything. Years ago I was on the train going to Darjeeling to make my annual retreat. And on the train I heard the voice of God telling me I was to serve *the poorest of the poor*, and in them to recognize God who is suffering.[5] That's the way of looking through or really seeing we must think about. We miss so much if we do not look for God beyond the surface."

Many studies and even our personal experience support Mother Teresa's words. We tend to take our ability to see for granted, and trust what we think we see as fact or reality. We rarely question our looking unless something takes us by surprise. And with this approach, we go through life missing out on so many opportunities. In "A Way of Seeing" Frederick Franck says,

> We do a lot of looking: we look through lenses, telescopes, television tubes...our looking is perfected every day...but we see less and less.
>
> Never has it been more urgent to speak of *seeing*. Ever more gadgets, from cameras to computers, from art books to videotapes, conspire to take over our thinking, our feeling, our experiencing, our seeing.... Quickly we stick labels on all that is, labels that stick once and for all. By these labels we recognize everything but no longer *see* anything....
>
> Millions of people, unseeing, joyless, bluster through life in their half-sleep, hitting, kicking, and killing what they have barely perceived. They have never learned to *see*, to experience....
>
> Looking and seeing both start with sense perception, but there the similarity ends.[6]

"My lepers taught me so much about this," Father Damien breaks in. "So many people were terrified of them, saw them as dangerous and threatening, maybe even the cause of their own sickness. They did not seem to look or see beyond the disease. And so they rounded them up, discarded them in a sense, on Molokai. On the big island I had already known several folks with leprosy before I agreed to go to the leper settlement and be the priest there. So it was no surprise to me to find them just like other people, only suffering so much now, not only because of their leprosy but also because of their separation from their families and friends. They were not worthless or disposable people. They became my family, many of them very, very dear to me."

"The problem is," Mother Teresa picks up, "that the way we 'see' things decides how we live, and usually we

only see what we have learned to see or what we have
gotten used to. How many times Jesus challenged us with
having eyes but not being able to see! How true that still
is in many ways. We do not realize that we have
something to say about what we see."

Mother Teresa's words echo the mystic Evelyn
Underhill who long ago spoke of the struggles to see
clearly in order to make contact with God as reality. "It is
notorious that the operations of the average human
consciousness unite the self, not with things as they really
are, but with images, notions, aspects of things."[7] And she
continues, "We throw a mist of thought between ourselves
and the external world: and through this we discern, as in
a glass darkly, that which we have arranged to see."[8]

What becomes apparent then is that whatever we see
can be interpreted or read in an infinite variety of ways.
The apostle Paul makes the same point, "...[B]ut we
proclaim Christ crucified, a stumbling block to Jews and
foolishness to Gentiles, but to those who are the called,
both Jews and Greeks, Christ the power of God and the
wisdom of God."[9] Blake illustrated our choices and habits
in seeing when he wrote that the fool sees not the same
tree as a wise man sees.

Psychology teaches that we never deal objectively
with anything. Through the ways we "see" we give birth
to and invent our reality as much as we find it. Rainer
Maria Rilke beautifully writes:

> ...there's a power in me
> to grasp and give shape to my world.
>
> I know that nothing has ever been real
> without my beholding it.
> All becoming has needed me.
> My looking ripens things
> and they come toward me, to meet and be met.[10]

This way of seeing—realizing our part in every encounter—allowed Damien to call his lepers, from whom most of society was running in horror, his dear children of God, and to spend his last sixteen years living with them, ministering to them. Though he regretted that his leprosy would cut short his life and ministry when there was still so much need, he also saw that his leprosy was "doing him the favor of shortening his road to heaven, and for that he thanked God and the Virgin Mary."[11]

> ...[W]hat we see and hear around us is at least as much our invention as it is our discovery; ...we contribute so much to the existence of the reality of the world we know that we can never separate what we create from what is already "out there." From this the next step inexorably follows: There are other ways of creating our contribution to what is real and thereby changing reality. The next step is even harder: We each have a responsibility for creating and maintaining the universe we live in; what the world is like is to a large—and as yet unknown—degree up to us.[12]

When we decide what something is—when we "see" it in a certain way—then we know how to deal with it. If a parent sees a tiny baby as a lovely gift of God, that parent will treasure the baby and treat her well. If the parent sees the baby as a burden, interrupting life plans and creating problems, chances are that parent would treat her poorly. When we "see" in certain ways and decide what our reality is, then we wind up dealing with that perception as fact, as if that vision is the only way things can be. We never stop and think that much of what we are dealing with is our own creation. For us, this is just the "way things are." How important, then, to question ourselves about how and what we "see."

Teresa and Damien speak clearly. They are direct—never mincing words, never sparing feelings, often challenging those around them. They do not challenge us to see the way they do, but to develop our own vision. They both grew up in a time when their Catholicism was strict and pietistic. Yet there is real congruence between what they see, what they say and what they do. Our times are different and yet similar. Their challenge to us is to truly believe the gospel, too, and bring it to life as we, uniquely, can.

We all live our lives from our own vision. The way we "see" is the deepest ground out of which we do all that we do. It is as though we each have a unique pair of glasses through which we look at life. Each of us created our own lenses, without even knowing we were doing so. We may have built in a certain way of looking because our parents looked at life that way. Sometimes a painful experience caused another particular focus—like the time things did not go the way we wanted and we felt "picked on" by life. An experience of rejection may have pushed us to see ourselves as unworthy. And so often everyone around us told us which people were admirable and which were useless, who deserved our love and care and who did not. We soon found that lots of us were wearing the same "glasses" and telling each other how right we were to "see" in such ways. Eventually, we did not even question if our way of seeing was accurate. It just was. Perhaps we never even questioned how our way of seeing arose, or where it came from.

"Seeing" or perceiving in any way is the first of our lessons from Teresa and Damien. If we do not see clearly, all that follows the seeing will be based on something false or misread. "Sometimes, to make progress past a certain point, we have to change the basic way we think about it...."[13]

Mother Teresa does not waver as the morning closes: *"The greatest sin is the absence of love and charity, the terrible indifference to our fellow man who, lying in the gutter, is exposed to exploitation, corruption, indigence, and disease.... If sometimes poor people have had to die of starvation, it is not because God didn't care for them, but because you and I didn't give, were not instruments of love in the hands of God; because we did not recognize him, when once more Christ came in distressing disguise..."*[14] So clearly she states the first misstep: "because we did not recognize him."

For Reflection

- *Are you willing to examine your way of seeing? How did it come about? What other ways of seeing are there? How do you take off the "glasses" you have been looking through and find those that give you God's vision? Perhaps you can, using the phrase "beginner's mind," look afresh at each thing as though it were something you have never seen before.*

- *How do you see God? If, as someone once said, there are as many Gods as there are people, who is your God?*

- *How do you see your own illness or condition? What do you tell yourself about it? What are some other ways you might describe it to yourself? How else can you think of it than the way you do? Maybe your own illnesses are not a punishment. Maybe they are the opening through which God can come into your life and be at home.*

- *What do you see in the illnesses or circumstances of others' lives? Can you see your own condition, or the pitiful condition of the AIDS patient, the homeless, the suffering in a new light?*

Closing Prayer

Like the blind man in the Gospel
O God, please help me to see!
Help me to recognize how much my seeing is my
    own responsibility. I want to remember that much
    of what I see in life is my own creation.
Because if I remember, then I'll stop to question
    myself and know I have a choice.
May my "seeing" and all my thoughts become more
    and more like yours.

Notes

[1] Isaiah 55:8.

[2] Mother Teresa, as quoted by Andrew Harvey, ed., in *The Essential Mystics: The Soul's Journey Into Truth* (San Francisco: HarperSanFrancisco, 1996), p. 214.

[3] Isaiah 53:2-3.

[4] Nobel Prize Address, Mother Teresa, as quoted in Serrou, p. 109.

[5] Gjergji, p. 34.

[6] Frederick Franck, "A Way of Seeing," in *Ordinary Magic: Everyday Life as Spiritual Path*, John Welwood, ed. (Boston: Shambhala, 1992), p. 80.

[7] Evelyn Underhill, *Practical Mysticism* (New York: Dutton, 1915), p. 5.

[8] Underhill, p. 34.

[9] 1 Corinthians 1:23-25.

[10] Rainer Maria Rilke, "*Da neigt sich die Stunde und rührt mich an,*" in *The Book of a Monastic Life*, translated by Anita Barrows and Joanna Macy in *Rilke's Book of Hours: Love Poems to God* (New York: Riverhead, 1996), p. 47.

[11] Daws, p. 200.

[12] Lawrence LeShan, *Alternate Realities* (New York: Ballantine, 1976), p. 3.

[13] LeShan, p. 4.

[14] Serrou, p. 76.

DAY TWO

In His Distressing Disguise

Coming Together in the Spirit

The Father General of a great monastic order began his visitation at a troubled monastery. Rancor, bitterness and criticism prevailed among the monks, with only traces of the Christian love expected in such a setting. In his first community session the General heard countless reports of the failings and grievances that many described as keeping them from the life for which they had come to the monastery. Monks were choosing to leave rather than live in this atmosphere of unkindness and distress.

Following a time of meditation and prayer, the General met with each monk individually. After their discussion, he ended each of these sessions with what he had found in prayer: "My dear brother," he told each monk, "in my plea for direction and blessings for this monastery, God gave me a special awareness. Jesus himself, out of a great desire to be with people again, has come back to earth and is living among you in this monastery. Needless to say, wanting to experience human life as you do, he is keeping his presence unobtrusive and quiet. May you be blessed abundantly in your good fortune and in your association with him."

Years later, no one could remember just when things changed at that monastery. They simply knew that it drew many men to holiness and became recognized as

one of the most desirable places to live—a house radiant
with Christian love.

Defining Our Thematic Context

Many of us instinctively withdraw from the sensual
onslaught of extreme human suffering. Do we respond in
similar ways when things are not so openly assaultive—
the family member or neighbor with AIDS or cancer, the
needy family down the street, our own failing selves?
These are the people and situations we do not have to go
to India or Molokai to find. These are the ones that
challenge us everyday, when we cannot plead lack of
airfare or time as our excuse. For these situations that are
so commonplace—too close to home to be special—we
have developed a way of seeing that protects us, that
allows us to avoid what is all around us. Are we even
willing to walk there, to look afresh into these
situations—at places and people we are sure we already
know?

On Day One of our retreat Father Damien and Mother
Teresa encouraged us to look anew at the way we see.
Instead of stopping off at the surface of life, a way station
that tends to ensnare most of us, they push us on into the
depths of the richness all around. They push us there
even when it is hidden behind fear, boredom,
sophistication, apparent failure, depression, poor choices,
or the muck of dirtiness, disease, unsightliness or even
death. They have told us that we will find God there.

Today they want to show us what that means for us.
They want to take us along with them as they move
through their next steps. If we are willing to see
differently, what will that mean? Instead of letting us stop
on the surface, or stay in our comfortable habits, they

want to show us the wealth we might find—as well as what it might cost us. To find Jesus "in his distressing disguise" means not only finding Jesus but also making our way through the distress of his disguise, which can demand more than we may think we can give.

Opening Prayer

Hidden God, you make it hard on us.
Here we are with our good intentions, wanting to
    reach out to "those" sorely needy people.
Thank you for that desire. You are the very source of
    that desire in us—a sure sign of your presence.
But we have so many good reasons why we cannot
    leave home and family to go to them. We are off
    the hook.

And then you come pointing to the sorely needy right
    where we live.
Help us to see them.
Help us to see that you are also here and often needy
In the poorly-dressed as well as in the richly-dressed,
In the hungry and dirty as well as in the overfed and
    well-groomed,
In the distressed as well as in the comfortable,
In the young as well as in the old,
In strangers as well as in family and friends,
In us as well as in the others.
And that is when you make it hard.
Because you are here.
We do not have to look anywhere else.

Retreat Session Two

They are already waiting for us, heads together as the sunlight streams through the windows behind them, obviously finding comfort in talking with each other about their experiences. As we take our seats and settle in around them, Teresa and Damien stop their conversation and welcome us with nods and smiles.

"Today might be a hard day," Father Damien begins, "so let's thank God for the beauty of it, the company and comfort we have with each other, and set about our program." (Damien lived by a schedule at Kalawao—his "Personal Rule" he called it. It was his way of keeping himself to the business at hand.)

He continues, "We talked yesterday about seeing more clearly, about refining our ways of seeing, and moving past the surface of what we see. There is a danger to that, you know. Because whenever we wake up and look with more awareness, we will certainly find something. And what we find will have two sides to it, just like everything else. Not only can we expect to find God, who is behind and within and around everything, we'll also find that God's beauty and greatness may not be obvious. God's presence is also within many people and things that will challenge us. That will cost us something."

"The cost to us," Mother Teresa adds, "is that once we know who it really is disguised in the needy people around us, we have to let go of our own comfort sometimes, our old ways of looking at life, our old ways of doing things, and spend ourselves for those who need us. This is never easy. We were created to love and to be loved, and he (Jesus) became man to enable us to love him as he loves us. He has become one with the hungry, the naked, the homeless, the sick, the persecuted, the lonely, the abandoned ones, and he tells us: 'You made me like this.' He hungers for our love, and this is the hunger that afflicts our poor people. *This is the hunger that every one of us ought to seek out. It might even be found in our own homes.*"[1]

"Mother Teresa," a youthful voice from our group reaches out tentatively, "I think you may have just answered a question of mine, but I want to be sure. Hearing about all that you do, and your sisters, and what you have done, too, Father Damien, I get all fired up and want to join both of you. I want to go off to India or to a place where there are so many suffering people and work with them and love them. But I have a husband and two little babies, and I know my responsibility is to them. But then I feel like I am not giving all I can, like I am missing the Jesus alive in those people who are hurting so."

Mother Teresa's voice is warm, "Ah, my daughter, *[w]hat is important is that God calls each one in a different way.*[2] Who would create and love and raise the children, who are such lovely gifts of God, if everyone was in the streets and hospitals with the suffering? That is why I mention the hunger you might find in your own homes, in the people who share life with you, and those you meet and work with. The same Jesus is hungry in all of them and so many times we look right past him.

"Sometimes the work is even harder in our own homes and neighborhoods because it is so mundane and everyday, and often these are people we know. It might surprise you, but it may be harder for us to love people we know than to love those who are strangers. Our intentions can be very good, but we might only look to be involved in the more dramatic situations. Then we are missing how green the grass is on our side of the fence, how much need there is right where we are.

"The hunger you meet in others might not be for physical things. Sometimes those are the easiest hungers to fill. We all have a hunger for God—for love—but often have strange ways of expressing it. We disguise our hunger and try to fill it up with things that will not last. Then we are hungry all over again. Drugs and shopping and workaholism and just plain 'busyness' can be distracting, but only temporarily. People may look very busy and very self-sufficient on the outside and be starving for meaning and love on the inside."

Clearly Mother Teresa is on a favorite subject. She seems on fire in her expression, filled with a glowing energy and excitement.

"So it seems our challenge is to respond to the way God calls each of us in our very individual concrete situations and lives. It is the call to see clearly the Jesus who is in your husband, your babies, those you work with, your neighbors, even the ones you do not especially like, even the ones who wrong you. And then, the call is with that same beautiful love and desire to serve Jesus in the poor, to move to fill the deep hungers of those close to home—hungers for love, for recognition, for someone to care about them and their lives, for a helping hand at times, for very down-to-earth attention.

"What about the times when you are exhausted with the millions of jobs that only a mother knows. You can hardly wait to get into bed, but just as you sink into sleep, one of the little ones has a frightening dream and screams for your arms to hold her. So you crawl out of bed and go to comfort her. I have often said we have to *give to each other until it hurts*.[3] Many mothers would not think of the pain involved in caring for their families because they are doing it out of love, but that is exactly what happens. That love does hurt sometimes. All love hurts sometimes. Whenever we are called to say no to ourselves, to our own comfort or desires in order to answer someone else's need, it hurts. It is hard for us to do that, but that is often the pain of loving."

All the while Mother Teresa is talking, Damien is leaning his head toward her, nodding every now and then, animated by her enthusiasm. Memories of his own efforts to meet the hungers and needs of the people he served—memories of building houses and churches, of changing bandages, preaching, touching misshapen hands and feet in the anointing of the sick, planting and harvesting the garden's bounty, sharing prayers with the dying and their families, digging graves, taking care of countless administrative tasks, seeing his lepers caring for each other—all bring tears to his eyes. Memories of so many ways of loving and serving have filled his life. He knows from experience how much need there is, how much hunger, and how close to each of us it lies, if we only have eyes to see.

But he is also aware that it is never easy to have such a way of seeing. The suffering and emotional scourging that came into his life as he went about loving and caring for his lepers were not part of his early dreams of missionary work. How well he knew now that no matter how lofty our dreams about loving and caring for those who are suffering, we will always wind up right in the middle of suffering ourselves in one form or another. Suffering came in so many different ways, there always seemed to be some of the hurt that Mother Teresa talked about. Not only was his work draining and physically hard, at times he was repulsed by the sights and smells that eventually became everyday experiences.

Charles Warren Stoddard, a visitor to Molokai, offered a description of a Sunday morning Mass with Father Damien presiding, that shows clearly both the wondrous gift of being able to serve as well as the difficulty that went with it:

> With gentle gravity, the priest began. The chapel
> was filled with the faithful, who joined in the
> singing with fervor and compunction. What a
> contrast! At the altar bright with lights and
> decorations, the priest in perfect health singing in a
> clear and sonorous voice the Preface and the Our
> Father. At his feet, acolytes with childish features
> marked by death. In the nave, an assemblage in
> which no face could be looked at without horror.
> The air was tainted, a fetid odor arose from those
> unfortunates who prayed so well. And I said to
> myself that such prayers, mounting to heaven
> through the mediation of such a servant of God,
> could not fail to be granted.[4]

Damien was thinking how hard he had to contend with
his own problems as he moved among the lepers. No
matter that he came with the best of intentions, his very
human nature rebelled against the sights and smells. He
remembered how he began to smoke his pipe to cover the
nauseating smells he encountered, how he had to get
outside into the fresh air sometimes in order to be able to
continue his visiting of those whose bodies were being
consumed with the ravages of leprosy.[5] No, it was not
easy. The cost to his very humanness was great.

> The smell of the crowd at St. Philomena's became so
> bad one day that he wanted to run outside; he
> stayed. At communion time, he was afraid he might
> not be able to swallow the consecrated wine and the
> Sacred Host for nausea; he managed to. "Sometimes,
> confessing the sick, whose sores are full of worms
> like cadavers in the grave, I have to hold my nose."
> But he stayed on in the confessional. And
> administering extreme unction to the dying, his own
> hands had to find a way to apply the consecrated oil
> to hands and feet that were nothing but open sores.[6]

Knowing that Jesus is present "in his distressing disguise" in each person in need provided the courage and support that kept Damien and Teresa on their paths. This is the Jesus who spoke clearly about what it meant to follow him and to enter into his kingdom, as we see in Damien and Teresa.

> When the Son of man comes in his glory, and all the angels with him, then he will sit on the throne of his glory. All the nations will be gathered before him, and he will separate people one from another as the shepherd separates the sheep from the goats. He will put the sheep at his right hand and the goats at the left. Then the king will say to those at his right hand, "Come, you that are blessed by my Father, inherit the kingdom prepared for you from the foundation of the world; for I was hungry and you gave me food, I was thirsty and you gave me something to drink, I was a stranger and you welcomed me, I was naked and you gave me clothing, I was sick and you took care of me, I was in prison and you visited me." Then the righteous will answer, "Lord, when was it that we saw you hungry and gave you food, or thirsty and give you something to drink? And when was it that we saw you a stranger and welcomed you, or naked and gave you clothing? And when was it that we saw you sick or in prison and visited you?" And the king will answer them, "Truly I tell you, just as you did it to one of the least of these who are members of my family, you did it to me."[7]

"Sometimes it is easy to see through his disguise," Damien says. "The little children were always special to me. And I am sure Mother Teresa would say the same thing about all the throwaway babies she has found in gutters and garbage cans. The little ones seem so simple and open. I remember one day when I was returning from an errand, *I came upon one of my little leper girls who asked me to bring her Holy Viaticum without delay. The acts of thanksgiving after Communion were scarcely finished when she gave her soul to God. With my own hands I made her coffin and dug her grave.*[8]

"With children the cost asked of us is not so obvious. They are so helpless, and we do not think of them as bringing anything on themselves. We seem more able to reach out to those we see as real victims. The cost becomes greater when we have to struggle with the repulsiveness or dirtiness of the person who needs our help, which is always hard. We so naturally want to turn away from them. But sometimes accepting their outer dirtiness is easier than battling all the internal judgments and criticisms, fears and rejections and prejudices we all carry within us about people who may be as much victims as the little ones. This can be so true about people we do not like, or those we disagree with or whose style of life is not what we think it should be.

"Asking us to find God in these people feels like asking too much of us. The cost is often too high. It is easier to hold on to our judgments about how they must have brought it on themselves, how they just want something for nothing, how they have to work for a decent life and should not expect us to do everything for them, how they are getting what they deserve—all kinds of ways we excuse ourselves from any responsibility to them."

"I'm starting to see something about myself here," a weak voice rises from the back of the group. All eyes turned toward the fragile-looking woman who had spoken. We had been aware of her, quietly huddled in her chair, sometimes shifting her position in obvious discomfort, her bones easily visible under her skin.

"Ever since my cancer came on, I am saying all those

same things about myself. I can be really caring of other people. I can be moved to tears by what some people are going through and really see Jesus in them. But when it comes to me, I don't think he is here. I know I must have deserved punishment for something, that I don't at all measure up to what I should be. I keep trying to find God in me, but my looking never finds anything except sadness and uselessness. I feel dead-ended. If in any way God is disguised in me, the disguise is perfect. I will never find him."

As the woman's voice grows weaker and stops on a note of despair, silence envelopes the room. We feel the truth of what she has said rumbling around in our own beings. One of the last places we tend to look for love or for God is in ourselves. Finding real love there turns out to be one of the biggest challenges in our lives. "You are amazing grace," Joan Baez said a long time ago, "You are a precious jewel—special, unrepeatable, fragile, tearful...." What a struggle to think so of ourselves! "Love others as you love yourself," Jesus said. How important it must be then to love ourselves! But we look the other way. Truly loving ourselves may be as rare as snow in July.

With a warm awareness of the pain in the woman's voice, the person beside her reaches out arms that gently surround the frail body. As tears course down the suffering woman's cheeks her neighbor says quietly, "I see God in you. I have seen through his disguise and have felt his presence in you all along. Maybe it is just that we have a hard time believing it about ourselves. Maybe we need to let go of the conditioning or that illusion that God could never love the likes of us. Well, I do not think we can decide what God cannot do. Maybe that is what our illnesses are all about—they push us to turn within and challenge us to find our God there.

"When we become the victims of life's troubles—

when we are sick, or poor or suffering in some way—so many of us tend to reproach ourselves strongly. We can come up with all kinds of explanations—that we must have done something wrong, that we deserve whatever punishment God brings us, that we are just not good enough. Maybe when we change our way of seeing, this is one of the places we find we have lots to let go of, lots of old ways of seeing that need release. This might be one of the costs Father Damien was talking about."

We begin talking about all the things we might be asked to let go of when we change to seeing in new ways. If we see Jesus in someone with AIDS, are we going to continue blaming the ill for the illness? If we see Jesus in homeless people, will we think of them as leeches on society? If we see Jesus in our own ailments and conditions, will we keep battling with and hating ourselves for being weak and in need?

The morning draws to a close as we became more and more aware that seeing God in ourselves and in others is at the root of everything. Our reaching out in love to those in great need could begin within ourselves and in our everyday world wherever we live. Molokai and Calcutta are all around us.

For Reflection

- *Name the people in the world that you would describe as Jesus in "his distressing disguise." Be specific.*

- *Who are the people that give you the most trouble, that you get most upset or angry about?*

- *In what specific ways are these people challenging you to change your ideas or your attitudes about them?*

- *Who are the people in your own environment that are the*

hardest to see God disguised in?

■ *One teacher of Buddhism describes an exercise in which we are to see everyone and everything in our immediate world as a Buddha figure, whose sole purpose for being in our lives is to bring us to enlightenment. We might adapt that exercise, visualizing Jesus in each person.*

Closing Prayer

O God of marvelous disguises,
How is it that I keep looking beyond you?
It's like I just do not get it, like I do not understand
  the rules of the game.
I keep expecting the spectacular (which you are!),
And you are here in the everyday (which, if I had
  eyes to see, I would see as the spectacular!).
Let me begin again today, and see you
In myself and my own unique life,
In those in my own household,
In my friends and neighbors,
In people I do not like very much,
In people of all colors and races, ages and genders,
In people of all life-styles, with all kinds of illnesses,
  hungers, needs and conditions.
I want to see you. I count on your help.

Notes

[1] Gjergji, p. 137.
[2] Gjergji, p. 39.
[3] Serrou, p. 109.
[4] Englebert, pp. 136-137.

[5] Daws, p. 83.
[6] Daws, p. 84.
[7] Matthew 25:31-40.
[8] Englebert, p. 125.

DAY THREE

There Is Nowhere Where God Is Not

Coming Together in the Spirit

A pious man who tried to live by God's will lived in a valley out in the country. One day a great rain came to his valley and the floodwater rose. The man went from the first floor to the second floor as the rains continued. Finally he climbed out onto the roof. A rescue boat came up and offered to tow him to safety, but the man sent them away saying, "I have full faith in God. I pray and believe and trust he will care for me." So the rowboat left. The storm continued, and soon the floodwater was up to his neck. A second rowboat came to rescue him and again was dismissed in the same way, "I have faith and trust in God. I pray and believe." So they left. It continued to rain and the water got so high that the man could barely breathe through his mouth and nose. A helicopter flew over and let down a ladder to rescue him. "Come up," they said, "we will take you to safety." "No," he cried with the same words as before, "I have faith in God. I pray and believe and I trust and I have followed him," he said, sending the helicopter away. It continued to rain, the waters rose and, finally, the man drowned.

He went to heaven and after a short period there was granted an interview with God. He expressed his

confusion: "I had so much faith in you. I believed in you
so fully. I prayed and tried to follow your will. I just do
not understand." At this point God scratched his head
and said, "I don't understand either! I sent you two
rowboats and a helicopter..."[1]

Defining Our Thematic Context

In God's great masquerade in this life, Damien and
Teresa could not be fooled. They were unswerving in
their efforts to see through masks and disguises, even the
most unlikely. In those who looked unattractive, even
repulsive—in the poor, the discarded, those suffering with
hideous diseases—and even in the powerful and well-to-
do, they recognized God and spent themselves in love for
such people.

They did not stop there. It was not only people in
whom God hid. Though they focused specifically on the
needy people they found, through their own experiences
they discovered God hiding and at work in all kinds of
places and situations. They knew they could not corner
God. They had to be open enough to spot him when he
crept out of corners and cracks both outside and inside
themselves. In today's session their experiences push us
to take all limits off God's disguises and open our minds
to great surprises.

Opening Prayer

Teresa, you found God in the smiles you offered the
        needy.
Damien, you found God in your own leprosy.
You both found God in a whole litany of life

experiences and situations.
Some were pleasant and enjoyable. Some were
painful and difficult.
What unexpected places God chooses!
Help us to believe that there is no place where God is
not.
That makes it easy.
We don't have to figure out which is which.
We just have to find God at work in every situation,
every circumstance,
In our own selves and our own lives and in the lives
of others.
Help us to become good seekers and good finders.

RETREAT SESSION THREE

Damien and Teresa enter the sunlit room together on
this third day, he leaning on her small frame for support,
she bearing up under his weight and smiling as they inch
toward their seats. The days are taking a toll on his failing
health, yet once settled in his chair, his misshapen face
radiates the delight he feels in sharing our experiences.
Mother Teresa's energy seems limitless.

"We've been talking about finding God in all the
people we meet," Mother Teresa begins. "Father Damien
and I want to stretch that into other places today. We also
want to explain ourselves a bit, because it would be easy
to stay with the words we have said during our lives and
not grow beyond them. And we have grown beyond
them!

"In our days, we tended to look on the world as a
place of exile, of suffering and sorrow. Heaven was our
aim. We just had to make it through life here, and if we

did, we would find our reward in heaven. That is the way we went about our missionary work. And of course, the people we cared for tended to be in such miserable condition that the thought of heaven and an eternal reward brought them some comfort and hope for solace and relief. We both found a lot of satisfaction in following those old traditional ways; we believed them so strongly. Standing back now, we know we can find and serve God in so many ways. We know that God is not only manifest in the poor and needy, and not only in people. Maybe that is what we must talk about today—expanding our awareness and our ability to find God."

Outside our wall of windows aspen leaves gleam in the brilliant morning sun, lighting and filling the room with golden warmth. Two magpies chatter and strut and flash their wings in their search for food. Our silence shows our eagerness to hear and learn what they came with today. One of the young nurses in the group speaks up.

"I think what you are saying about stretching our awareness of God's presence into all kinds of places is sort of what I try to do. When I have the privilege of caring for very sick people, I have a way of thinking about them that helps me a lot. Not only do I try to see God in them as persons, I also think about how God might be at work in them—for their sake as well as for mine. I am not saying that God caused their illness, but I do believe that God works through their illness, offering something to them and to me as I care for them."

If God is present in every situation and circumstance of life, since it is in God that "we live and move and have our being,"[2] then the illness itself can speak to us, heavy as it is with all kinds of literal and symbolic meaning. Even the experience of the illness has something to say to us.

Thomas Moore sends us off in this direction. "All

illness is meaningful, although its meaning may never be translatable into entirely rational terms. The point is not to understand the cause of the disease and then solve the problem, but to get close enough to the disease to restore the particular religious connection with life at which it hints."[3] Since "all things work together for good,"[4] our illnesses, as well as all other life experiences, even those we see as negative, may provide a rich source of contact with God. In *The Alchemy of Illness*, Kat Duff, reflecting on her own illness, writes, "Then, as I was falling asleep that night, it occurred to me that my illness is my spiritual path and practice—at least for now."[5]

The nurse continues, "It may be in the way the patient deals with her illness that I can find a gift for me. A person I am caring for may be very impatient. What I do then is to try to figure out what I need to learn about patience myself. If the patient is angry and fighting the illness, I look at the way I try to handle things I do not want in my own life. I pray in every situation to be open to whatever the lesson is, and realize that God brought the two of us together for some reason. I do not want to miss the gift that is there for me in our encounter. So I see God not only *in* the person, but also working *through* the illness and every other aspect of the situation."

"Do you mean," the frail woman who spoke yesterday interrupts, "if I were your patient that you would see God working through me? Even through my awful cancer? Through my irritation and my despair? Even when I do not feel like God is anywhere near? Even when I feel very angry with God?"

The young nurse nods her head. "I'm afraid so."

"Why should this be such a surprise?" Father Damien interjects. "In the Holy Saturday liturgy we speak of '*felix culpa*,' 'happy fault,' our human failings that brought us a savior. Why do we think our own individual failings and problems and illnesses would not also be places where God will come? In our broken places, when we have cracks in our usual armor, an opening is created where God can enter. Otherwise we do not even know our need and wind up sealing ourselves off and thinking we can take care of everything ourselves.

"Now, as I think about it, God was in the needs of my parishioners, even in those people who were not Catholics, calling me to come to their help. It was God working through their suffering, who asked me to open myself to whatever way they needed help. It was God calling my name, who pulled me out of myself to stretch me in a million different directions, and showed me so many ways in which I could serve that were beyond my wildest imaginings.

"I went to the missions because I wanted to do God's work. I had no idea when I set out what that eventually would come to mean for me. In my dreams and hopes I just was eager to be a missionary priest *running night and day over the volcanoes of the islands in search of strayed sheep.*[6] But I quickly found out that life on the islands asked many things of me that were somewhat less glamorous than that early picture.

"God has a way of coming at us from all angles, it seems, even asking for service and caring from us in things for which we feel ill-prepared. I had always worked hard with my hands since I was a young boy, so the building and repairing of the church and houses and garden work—even digging graves—all came easily to me. But then I had to find God in the administrative work that I was asked to do, and in the medical care that sometimes seemed more than I could handle. I had never done those things before, but I gave them my best and eventually could do what was needed."

"The last thing I was looking for," Mother Teresa joins

in, "was to have to go and receive the honors and public attention that came to me for the work I was doing. My vocation, as I saw it, was just to care for the poorest of the poor. But my doing that brought out all kinds of other things I did not expect. People asked me to talk about my work. At first I resisted—I did not want to be the center of attention. I did not think God wanted me to be in the public eye. But it came to me that God was asking me to speak for the needy, for the poor and suffering who could not speak for themselves. I could make their needs known in ways they could not. I could be a voice for them and bring their plight to the attention of the world. And whatever gifts or awards came to me through these talks I received in their name and for their needs."

According to these stories, God was disguised in an amazing number of ways and kept popping up everywhere! No matter the need, God is in it somewhere, challenging us to see, surprising us at every turn.

A scrim is a piece of stage scenery on which the background of a set is painted. When lit from the front, it is opaque and creates the illusion of being whatever the play demands: a wall, a street, a mountain range, a view of paradise. But when lit from behind, it becomes transparent, almost invisible, and the actual stage behind it can be seen.

> This world is like a scrim, a temporary creation, beyond which can be seen the stage on which (at another time) other plays will be mounted and other actors will perform their parts. We tend to see the world as if it were solid, permanent, and substantial. Seen through the eyes of Truth, however, it becomes transparent. When our vision pierces the scrim, we begin to see life as it is, through the eyes of the Creator. Only then can we view the real universe.[7]

However, it is rarely clear what we are being asked to see

and do in a given situation. We need healthy discernment. We must ask, "How is God at work here? What exactly is God asking of me? What response is the loving response?"

Neither Damien nor Teresa would advocate an unthinking or blind assent to anything in our lives simply because we believe God is there. Some discernment is always called for. In their own lives they recognized situations they believed displeased God and made attempts to change them. They worked to be clearly aware of what God was asking.

Both were traditional Catholics, rigorous and self-disciplined in their practices and beliefs. Yet neither of them rejected the beliefs of others, or rejected any others because of their beliefs and religious practices. They knew there was no place where God was not, and so showed us that no one way of being could capture God. We can find God wherever we are willing to look with our own unique ways of looking, through our own perspectives.

Lest we think that the assurance of God's presence in any situation called forth a cheerful Pollyanna response from our mentors, we must see the whole picture—both Damien and Teresa were people like us, struggling at times with who they were and what life was presenting. They were plainspoken and could even be harsh when their censure was called for. Damien told of adjusting his own style to meet the needs of each person in his care. *"Almost from one house to the next I have to change my tone. Here, I give words of sweetness and consolation, there, I mix in a little bitterness, because it is necessary to open the eyes of a sinner, finally, the thunder sometimes rumbles, and I threaten an impenitent with terrible punishments, which often produces a good effect."*[8]

When Damien encountered immoral behavior he did not hesitate to confront people, leaving no question of his displeasure. He got especially upset about the members of the leper colony who had chosen lives of promiscuity and debauchery. "Damien was known to invade the dance house, hefting the walking stick he carried, to break up the dances, scattering performers and overturning the drinking calabashes."[9] Needless to say, some people were angry with him and offended by his interruption of their pleasures. He, however, believed he was bringing God into a situation where others were trying to keep him out.

Teresa, too, was straightforward when she found situations not to her liking. She would plainly speak her mind, and kept tight control over her missionaries and their services. She and Damien both had their critics, but took on the guise of outspoken prophets who did not worry about softening their words when they had something to say. Mother Teresa's forthright criticism of a society that often held back its love and care for those in need, and her unflinching abhorrence of abortion, among other things, led one magazine article to note that she "lacked the humility of self-doubt." Some people were put off simply by her strict and unbending style. Yet no one could find fault with her loving attention to the poor.

For many of us, the rougher aspects of Teresa's and Damien's personalities provide a bit of comforting contrast to their totally committed and giving lives. Their more evident faults and quirks make them seem more human. This removes our inclination to judge them as so far beyond us—even in a different category of humanness than we are—that we could never follow their examples. Holding to such a belief exonerates us from our responsibility for those in need.

Perhaps it is this aspect of Teresa and Damien—the chinks in their ordinary humanity—that allows us to see God in them, and even endear them to us. If two notably imperfect persons can give so profoundly of themselves and have such a great impact on the lives of so many suffering people, then how can we excuse ourselves from the mandate that we, too, find God there? After all, God was disguised even in their idiosyncrasies and in ways beyond what we expect. Sometimes it is the absence of a trait we value that strengthens that trait in ourselves.

One of those absences in Damien and Teresa seems to be in their indifference to the natural world. Damien lived in a lush garden setting, surrounded by the deep blues of ocean and sky, rugged mountains, tropical flowers and towering waterfalls. Teresa covered the world in her travels, moving through spectacular settings of great natural beauty. They were both disinclined to comment on any of this. The natural world appeared simply unnoteworthy. Today, as we try to find God everywhere, we might look first to the beauty of creation. Our generation is more inclined to agree with Gerard Manley Hopkins, who notes in one of his most loved poems, "The world is charged with the grandeur of God."[10]

As the conversation about seeing God in all things winds to a close, Damien's eyes are dreamily gazing on the scene beyond the windows. The sun is climbing in the morning sky and the golden warmth permeates the crystal clarity of the windows. Silence falls over the group, each lost in thought. Mother Teresa shifts in her chair and yet stays with the group in the quiet. Finally one of the participants pulls out a journal and reads to the group from Thomas Merton:

> Life is this simple. We are living in a world that is absolutely transparent, and God is shining through it all the time. This is not just a fable or a nice story. It is true. If we abandon ourselves to God and forget ourselves, we see it sometimes, and we see it maybe frequently: God shows Himself everywhere, in

everything—in people and in things and in nature and in events. It becomes very obvious that God is everywhere and in everything and we cannot be without Him. It's impossible. The only thing is that we don't see it.[11]

For Reflection

- *How is God shining through your world right now? Think of the places or ways God's presence can be easily apparent to you.*

- *What are the places, or situations in your world where you never think of God as being present?*

- *Look at the trees, grass, plants and pets you encounter every day and speak to God present in them.*

- *Think about your own physical health, illness or disability. How does it speak to you of God? How is that experience part of your spiritual path?*

- *Sit quietly with your journal and begin to note the presence of God in your experiences.*

- *Determine to build an experience of delight in God's creation into your everyday life.*

Closing Prayer

O God who is closer to me than I am to myself,
Open my eyes and my mind and my heart to you and
   your presence all around me.
Show me how to accept you within me.
I get so busy, so caught up in things that are not
   important.

I tend to feel so alone, like no one understands or
knows me.
And all the while you are right here, waiting for me
to notice.
May I see my failings, my illnesses and my
experiences as places where you are.
May I see each one as a stepping stone on my
spiritual journey. Let me see that you are with me.
Every day let me see your face in the sky, in my
surroundings, in all your gifts.

Notes

[1] Christina Feldman and Jack Kornfield, eds., *Stories of the Spirit, Stories of the Heart: Parables of the Spiritual Path from Around the World* (San Francisco: HarperCollins, 1991), p. 278.

[2] Acts 17:28.

[3] Thomas Moore, *Care of the Soul* (New York: HarperCollins, 1992), p. 168.

[4] Romans 8:28.

[5] Kat Duff, *The Alchemy of Illness* (New York: Pantheon Books, 1993), p. 91.

[6] Letter to parents in Daws, p. 35.

[7] James Fadiman and Robert Frager, *Essential Sufism* (San Francisco: HarperSanFrancisco, 1997), p. 45.

[8] Daws, p. 85.

[9] Daws, p. 112.

[10] Gerard Manley Hopkins, "God's Grandeur" in *A Hopkins Reader* (New York: Image, 1966), p. 47.

[11] Quoted in Marcus Borg, *The God We Never Knew* (San Francisco: HarperSanFrancisco, 1997), p. 47.

DAY FOUR
Blessed Are the Poor

Coming Together in the Spirit

There were two monks who lived together for forty years and never argued. Not even once. One day, one said to the other, "Don't you think it's time we had an argument, at least once?"

The other monk said, "Fine, let's start! What shall we argue about?"

"How about this piece of bread?" said the first monk.

"Okay, let's argue about this bread. How are we going to do it?" said the second.

The first said, "This bread is mine; it belongs to me."

The second said, "If it is, take it."

Peace is not necessarily destroyed by a quarrel or an argument. It is the "I" that destroys peace. This is mine, and I don't want to split it with anyone. When you take such an attitude of attachment and selfishness, your heart gradually becomes harder and harder. This is the great enemy of peace: a heart that is attached, hardened, and selfish.[1]

Defining Our Thematic Context

We seem to walk through life wearing a coat of Velcro. Everything reaches out in an attempt to cling to us. Gifts of all kinds surround us and we quickly discover how easy it is to cover ourselves with an unending variety of things. Many of these gifts that become "ours" grow precious to us, and give us comfort and security. We think they even tell us who we are. So we snuggle into the thickening coat that encircles us as our possessions cling to us and buffer the harsher realities of life.

Interestingly, we rarely say "enough." Satisfaction eludes us though we continue to surround ourselves with so much that we think will bring contentment. As the Buddha said, desire is endless, and is the chief cause of our suffering.[2] This craving and accumulation of more than necessities in life provokes an enormous imbalance in the distribution of the world's goods. Those who "have" want to acquire more, leaving those who "have not" less than what they need.

Mother Teresa was unwavering in her indictment of this imbalance. *"Poverty is the creation of you and me,"* she once said, *"a refusal to share with others. God did not create poverty. He created only us. The problem will not go until we are able to give up greed."*[3] And she did not mean just material poverty. Just as we can acknowledge our clinging and greed in ways beyond the material, Mother Teresa also pushed us to consider the ways we meet poverty in our world, often as a result of the very abundance we experience. *"Suffering and poverty are found everywhere. And it is not only material poverty I speak of, for spiritual suffering and misery are constantly growing."*[4]

Today, Teresa and Damien invite us to approach poverty from two perspectives. First they dare us to reach out to those in need, whose poverty—in whatever form—is accompanied by suffering. These are the people who call to us and challenge our ability to love. Second, they encourage us to examine our own accumulation of internal and external trappings—attachments that mask the emptiness, the space in us where we can connect with and receive all that God offers us.

Opening Prayer

> O God, you fill the world with your goodness and
>   love.
> But somehow, we rearrange things.
> What you give as symbols of your love,
> What you give in abundance,
> What you mean for us to share,
> We cling to and hoard and keep from each other,
>   making them our gods.
> When we fill up and surround ourselves with what is
>   meant to be only the wrappings of you,
> No room is left in us for you.
> Let me begin afresh.
> Let me gratefully receive your gifts with open hands.
> Let them flow through me, opening up a warm and
>   loving space where you are,
> Blessing me and all those with whom I share you.

RETREAT SESSION FOUR

Mother Teresa's eyes are shining and bright as glowing coals. She is ready for the day. When we walk in the door of our meeting room her energy radiates and envelopes us. Her whole demeanor radiates fire. While Father Damien sits quietly in his chair, she darts around the room, encouraging later arrivals to their seats. The atmosphere is charged with electricity.

"Today we talk about poverty," she begins without preamble. Nothing seems to light Mother Teresa's eyes like her love for the poor. If she was extravagant in any respect, it was in her great commitment to the poor. This seemed to be the central focus of her life and the many that follow her. This was the center of her vocation. She loved quoting Mahatma Gandhi whose beautiful statement echoed her own belief, *"He who serves the poor, serves God."*[5]

It was her strong love for the poor that provoked her to overcome her aversion to so much publicity, so many awards and honors. She decided to accept the honors in the name of the poor, in their stead. It was her way of bringing them the recognition and dignity and distinction she believed they deserved. It also offered her a public forum which she used well. *"I don't know why universities and colleges are conferring titles upon me. I never know whether I should accept or not; it means nothing to me. But it gives me a chance to speak of Christ to people who otherwise may not hear of him."*[6]

Teresa and Damien had agreed that today would be hers. He would add his thoughts here and there, but like Francis of Assisi—one of her heroes—she would speak for the poor out of her boundless love, out of so much time spent with them.

"Many, many challenges come to us from the poor," she begins again. "Jesus was very clear. If he had any favorites in all the people he encountered, it was those who were poor. Let there be no misunderstanding or lack of awareness here. This is what the Church means when we speak of having a 'preferential option for the poor.'"

Walter Wink emphasizes the same concern and also cites others: "In his beatitudes, his healings, and his table fellowship with outcasts and sinners, Jesus declares God's special concern for the oppressed. God sides with the poor, not because of their virtue, but because of their suffering, not because of their goodness, but because they have been sinned against."[7]

"We do not have to go far to find the poor," Mother Teresa continues. "They appear in so many forms it is impossible to count them all. Most obvious are those living on the minimal amounts of this world's goods—right in our midst. These are people all around who cry out to us every day. We have become almost oblivious to their presence, studiously looking right past them as they grow in number and need. We have developed a way of keeping them from affecting us by creating a sort of place in our minds for them where we can ignore them. When we keep them in their place, with all the judgments we assign to them so we can exonerate ourselves, we do not have to acknowledge any responsibility for them and their condition. We think they do not deserve our love. *I believe the people of today do not think that the poor are like them as human beings. They look down on them. In fact, the poor have as much right to the things of life and of love as anybody* [8] does.

"Poor people feel nonexistent, valueless, humiliated," Walter Wink said. "No one takes notice of them, unless their votes are needed by the rich—in which case, likely as not, they even vote against their own self-interest. They often have little confidence in themselves, and actually believe that the rich know what they need better than they.... So deep is this internalized oppression that Gustavo Gutiérrez has based a wholly new task for theology upon it: not helping the bourgeois discover the 'meaning of life,' but assisting the dehumanized to recover their humanity."[9]

"Mother Teresa, I want to say something about that,"

Father Damien breaks in. "I am glad you said it is not only the materially poor that we are talking about. All that you said can apply to my lepers, too, and to many sick people. Still more people find themselves treated without much respect—those that are poor in influence, poor in knowledge and education, poor in health and those who are in their old age."

"You are right," Teresa replies, "we must not stop with the materially poor. We may find that, besides those you mention, there may be others who are poor. Many who look the most 'filled up'—the most well-fed, richly clothed, moneyed, admired and important—may lack an experience of real value in their lives. What makes these people even poorer is their lack of awareness that what they have, on which they have placed so much significance, is actually of no value. None of what is important to them is lasting."

"I see people that fit into some of those categories all the time," a hospital nurse offers. "We rush people through our medical system when they are sick. We get so caught up in all the technology that sometimes we miss the people we are using the technology on. We have depersonalized our care so much that you almost cannot call it care anymore. We treat patients like things. We are so busy we do not even speak to them as people. And older people seem to receive some of the poorest treatment."

Some in the group begin telling their own experiences of impersonal treatment by caregivers and many others, and even in some places of business. Because they did not look like they had a great deal of money to spend, they were ignored.

"In our families and acquaintances, in our neighbors and those we meet at work," Mother Teresa continues, "we often find other faces of poverty. There may be a real lack of human warmth, or any sense of being loved and understood. So many people say they have no one to listen to them, to care about them and what life is like for them—what their struggles are. We miss meeting each other and are all the poorer for it."

One of the group tells of an elderly gentleman she knew who had taken his longtime companion dog to the veterinarian to be euthanized for an incurable and painful illness of old age. After lovingly supporting his dog friend's departure from this world, the man went home and took his own life. A note was left to explain his decision. "This was the only other living creature who cared about me in this world, and I don't see how I could go on without him." This is one form of poverty in our world of loneliness.

"Maybe, Mother Teresa," a quiet member of our group ventures, "the first thing we might do is begin to be aware, to notice and name the poverty around us, all the ways we, and others, might be poor. But being poor, I think, means being without something we need, not just something we wish we could have. I think of everyday needs, like food and shelter and clothing."

One of the men speaks up, "We cannot just limit it to material things, though. Mother Teresa, you have spoken about the poor as being hungry for love, and said that perhaps the same hunger is in the people in our own homes.[10] You have said *the greatest injustice against the poor is to deprive them of their dignity.*[11] When you mentioned before how we look right past them, I thought about what I inflict on others when I do that—I send the message that they do not even exist, that they are not worthy of my attention, even my smile!"

How quiet the room becomes. Some of us shift around uncomfortably in our chairs, each lost in personal remembrances and experiences.

"I spend some of my time with the poor who are sick, and some that are dying," another participant says, breaking into the silence. "I was just thinking about how many different ways poverty can show up in the same person or same situation. As a hospice volunteer, I helped in a home where the husband and father was dying. He had been a strong and able man who had supported his family well. Then as he began to feel ill and miss work, the bottom dropped out of his world. He lost his job. He had a quickly growing cancer. In such a short time he seemed to lose almost everything he'd had. You might not call it poverty, but I saw him nearly despairing about what his life now held—he was without strength, without any sense of ability, he felt he was worth nothing to his family or himself and was only a burden. He felt abandoned by God, and could make no sense of anything. His family did not know what to do, did not even know how to talk to him—they began avoiding him. Even his friends seemed to stay away. In so many ways he seemed so poor to me."

"You see," Mother Teresa offers, "when we allow ourselves to look more clearly, we might be overwhelmed with what has been close to us all along. Once we start owning up to the real hunger and need all around us, we see that even in the richest of countries the poor are with us in so many guises. We can even look at our own experiences of illness and need and see how they made us so vulnerable and hungry for love and care. When we see how much need there is we know we have a big decision to make—what are we going to do about it?"

"Well, it seems to me," a nurse jumps in, "that we have to sort out the kinds of poverty and brainstorm what we can do. We certainly cannot lump them all together. Like, for a starter, there are some very real basic needs we can meet if we are open enough with our own material possessions. Everything in our world today seems to center around greed, around always wanting and having more."

Mother Teresa nods. *"The problem will not go until we are able to give up greed.*[12] *Let us not be satisfied with just giving money. Money is not enough, money can be got, but they need your hearts to love them."*[13]

Thomas Merton wrote a similar message in his journals:

> There is a distinction between charity, the theological virtue, and charity a modern word meaning a mechanical and impersonal kind of almsgiving, as, for example, when a millionaire leaves all his money to "charity." The poor will be always there for this kind of almsgiving, where the rich man, infinitely distant from the poverty of the poor, scratches with a pen on paper and starts a long series of book-keeping entries and abstract transactions which ends up a long time later with a nervous little social worker scolding a group of little kids who are trying to play baseball in a fenced-in gravel plot in a slum, somewhere.
>
> Without love, almsgiving is no more important an action than brushing your hair, or washing your hands, and the Pharisees had just as elaborate a ritual for those things as they had for alms, too, because all these things were prescribed by law, and had to be done so. But love does not give money, it gives itself. If it gives itself first and a lot of money too, that is all the better. But first it must sacrifice itself.[14]

Mother Teresa always brought attention to the need for love at the root of any giving. But while love remained primary, she welcomed the material gifts that eased the lives of the poor. She lived close to the poor herself and insisted that she and her sisters live like the poor, owning only what they needed. Damien's life reflected a similar willingness to be close to those who had little and to share his own possessions. "Damien...would eat anything or nothing; he gave away most of his clothes, and mended what was left with whatever was at hand: hot wax paper, and string, on one occasion."[15]

Walter Wink discussed the strong messages John the Baptist and Jesus taught about those who have and those who have not.

> John the Baptist set the tone for everything that was to follow: "Whoever has two coats must share with anyone who has none; and whoever has food must do likewise."(Luke 3:11)... Jesus, for his part, pours scorn on those who are clothed in soft raiment and dwell in king's houses (Matthew 11:8 and Luke 7:25). He challenges creditors, not only to forgo interest, but to ask no repayment whatever. To those who wish to follow him, he counsels selling everything, and warns the rich that they have no access whatever to the new society coming. Those who hoard luxuries and neglect the poor at their doors are presented with the prospect of their own death and divine judgment. To the religionist's dream of being able to be "spiritual" and still amass wealth within an unjust system, Jesus pronounces an unconditional no: "You cannot serve God and wealth."[16]

"It does not sound like there is much room in those ideas to waffle around!" our outspoken nurse picks up. "I know it is not just giving things, though, that is important. I hope we can interpret what those ideas mean in a broader sense, too. Like recognizing that when we are not cluttered with and clinging to lots of things, we can zero in on what is important in life. We can see better what really matters, like we have been talking about. And that is where love comes in, giving ourselves."

"And that takes us to the other aspects of poverty,"
Mother Teresa says, "the ways people who have so much
material good can be really poor and what we can do
about that. *I found the poverty of the West so much more
difficult to remove. When I pick up a person from the street,
hungry, I give him a plate of rice, a piece of bread, I have
satisfied. I have removed that hunger. But a person that is shut
out, that feels unwanted, unloved, terrified, the person that has
been thrown out from society— that poverty is so hurtable and
so much, and I find that very difficult.... You must come to
know the poor, maybe our people here have material things,
everything, but I think that if we all look into our own homes,
how difficult we find it sometimes to smile at each other, and
that the smile is the beginning of love. And so let us always
meet each other with a smile, for the smile is the beginning of
love, and once we begin to love each other naturally we want to
do something.*"[17]

"One more aspect seems important to me," a voice
comes from the rear. "I find that the less I cling to things,
the more I detach myself from things, the freer I feel and
the freer I am. That's when I feel less bogged down. I
might say that when I become poor inside myself—even
letting go of ideas and attitudes I've thought were so
important—the more I know I've got room for God to
come in. And the more room I have for other people, too.
I've come to see how important it is to be empty of so
much that doesn't matter. It's like I've shaken off a coat
that was keeping me restricted and caught in a web of
unimportant things. I can stand free and unencumbered
in the world."

We can see that Mother Teresa has given herself
completely to our discussion and understanding of
poverty and how important it is in each of our lives. She
sits down and with a pensive look on her face, listens as
the give and take rumbles on around her.

For Reflection

- *What is weighing you down, keeping you encumbered?*

- *What is there within you that you could release that would free you up and open your heart to God's poor?*

- *Can you identify the poor around you—not only the materially poor, but those with poverty of heart and spirit?*

- *What do you do for the poor of the world?*

- *In what ways are you poor? Do you recognize the ways God fills your needs?*

- *Why do you think that Jesus and the Church have a "preferential option for the poor"? What does that mean? What does it mean for you personally?*

Closing Prayer

O God of such great abundance that you outdo our
    wildest imaginations,
Clarify our way of seeing so we know what "riches"
    really are. May we let your riches flow through us
    to be shared with everyone.
May we never cling to what you provide for us, or
    think we "earned" it.
Your riches are free gifts, given to us with love.

May we find those who are poor all around us:
    those poor in spirit,
    those without basic necessities,
    those who receive the love of no one,
    those in our own homes and surroundings who
      lack real love,
    those sick and suffering with no one who cares.
May our hearts and hands always be open to share

our abundance with them.
In our giving, you continually fill us with yourself.
We would be so poor without you.

Notes

[1] Anthony DeMello, *Walking on Water* (New York: Crossroad, 1998), p. 21.

[2] Robert C. Lester, "Buddhism: The Path to Nirvana" in *Religious Traditions of the World*, H. Byron Earhart, ed. (San Francisco: HarperCollins, 1993), p. 908.

[3] Serrou, p. 75.

[4] Gjergji, p. 69.

[5] Serrou, p. 75.

[6] Serrou, p. 86.

[7] Albert Nolan, *God in South Africa*, quoted in Walter Wink, *Engaging the Powers* (Minneapolis: Augsburg Fortress, 1992), p. 112.

[8] Serrou, p. 77.

[9] Gustavo Gutiérrez, *A Theology of Liberation*, quoted in Wink, pp. 101-102.

[10] Serrou, p. 109.

[11] Serrou, p. 73.

[12] Serrou, p. 75.

[13] Serrou, p. 100.

[14] Patrick Hart, O.C.S.O., ed., *Run to the Mountain: The Journals of Thomas Merton, Volume 1, 1939-1941* (San Francisco: HarperCollins, 1995), p. 156.

[15] Daws, p. 219.

[16] Wink, p. 114.

[17] Serrou, p. 113.

DAY FIVE
Desolate Places

Coming Together in the Spirit

The request came at the end of a busy day, from a doctor on his way out of the hospital. "Joan, could you run by and see a patient of mine before you go home? We found cancer yesterday—something we had not expected—and it was a shock to her. She is an older woman, nice lady. She has gotten very quiet and is not saying much to me today, so I am not sure what is going on."

The darkening room was tinged with the orangy-rose glow of an Albuquerque sunset as I pushed open the door. From over the bed a light circled the frail figure nestled in blankets and cast shadows on the picked-over food on the dinner tray before her. The bustle and voices of the hallway faded into silence as the door closed behind me. Her doctor had told her I would come by. She was waiting and reached out her hand. "Will you sit here close to me?"

Conversation about the coming of death, while sometimes direct and focused, often circles and winds and creeps up on concerns, wanting to avoid any more harshness than what the facts already hold. And so did this one go as we touched on and examined so many tender places in her growing awareness of how shortened life had become. She felt devastated, threatened, scared.

And then she said, "I think I have been a wolf in sheep's clothing."

"I wonder what that means?" I softly questioned aloud.

Her answer came quickly, often a sign it had been lurking close to the surface. "I have always believed you get out of life what you put into it," she began. "And I thought I was putting in good things. But I guess I wasn't. I guess I've been fooling myself, or this would not have happened to me."

Defining Our Thematic Context

Many of us carry a belief that if we go about doing good we should not have to suffer. We assume that suffering is punishment, that it comes, just as we learned when we were children, to chastise us, to teach us a lesson, to make us "pay" in some way. If we are good there will be no need for punishment. Carrying this reasoning to its illogical conclusion tells us that as long as we live a good life, breaking none of God's commandments, we will not have to suffer or die.

Teresa and Damien tell us otherwise. If we subscribe to the belief that doing good exonerates us from suffering, certainly Damien and Teresa would have been exempt. Both stretched themselves beyond the point to which the vast majority of humans go to care for those suffering and in great need. Yet both of their lives, full of suffering, paint a different picture than this belief would suggest. Life misses no one in its relentless cycling through light times and dark times, through ups and downs— constantly moving toward life through death.

Today they want to walk with us in our struggles with the harsh and desolate times we experience. They both know this landscape and want to tell us that these times are as natural and expected as the sun rising and setting each day, and that we must never lose heart.

Opening Prayer

O God, in the beginning you created the earth with
   darkness and light,
And when you were finished you saw that everything
   was very good.
Cycling through the light and darkness of life carries
   delight and also harshness.
It carries growth and diminishment, times that we
   love and times that we suffer.
And we have no control over the movement.
It is simply your pattern—the way things are.

We also create light times and dark times
For ourselves and for each other.
We can bring blessings to those around us
And we can be devastatingly harsh.
We can build up.
We can tear down.
And we know the experience of receiving loving gifts
   as well as harsh rejection.

Walk with us through our desolate places.
Remind us that there is no place where you are not.
Wake us up to the fact that we cannot avoid the dark
   times,
That they are part of all life here.
May we never purposely be the source of harsh times
   for others,
And may we see our own harsh times as fertile soil
   for growth and love.

Retreat Session Five

Pounding rain rattles the windowpanes as thunder rumbles and lightning flashes. Nothing about the rain, grayness and heavy clouds invites us outdoors. We will be kept inside today, warm and dry.

Father Damien's head is sunken to his chest, his hands in his lap, his body and spirit withdrawn, engrossed in thought. His eyes, usually so full of joy and energy despite his ailing body, look bleak and listless. When Mother Teresa comes in she sits by him, and takes her chair quietly, a bit subdued. He wakes to her presence and a brief warm smile softens his face.

"I am not feeling well today," Damien begins. "Just like the weather I am sort of dark and gloomy." Mother Teresa reaches over and touches his misshapen hands. How many times she had been there when someone suffered, when all she could do was touch them lovingly and let them know they were loved. She had read somewhere that Damien had suffered what he called "black thoughts" during his years of ministry.[1]

In fact, Damien suffered desolation and the dark side of life in a number of ways. Even before he contracted leprosy, he struggled with feelings of unworthiness and melancholy. Despite all his care for his flock, all his efforts to provide whatever was needed for those suffering, all his prayer and self-discipline, Damien could not shake the feeling that he was unworthy of heaven. It tormented him.

From his early days in Kohala, he suffered from isolation, pleading with his superiors to send him a priest companion with whom he could share the ministry and to whom he could confess. But most of his life in Hawaii was spent alone.

It was too long, and Damien said so many times. Ordinary conversation with someone other than a Hawaiian, and confession, made to a fellow member of his Congregation—these were essential to the renewal of the spirit, the warding off of those black thoughts, that "insupportable melancholy." "...*Please plead the cause of the isolated priest of Kohala...it is too hard to go on like this*" [he wrote].[2]

"Today," Mother Teresa begins, "I think we must talk about these hard times—the times that assault all of us on the journey of our lives. Father Damien and I found we were not passed over by difficulties, nor did we expect to be. We had to work hard to see God's presence in both the delightful and the hard times. The Book of Isaiah says it well:

I form light and create darkness,
I make weal and create woe;
I the LORD do all these things.[3]

"I have learned," Damien says, "that we all go up and down in life, that everything alive in life goes in cycles. But even though I know that, it has still been very hard. Some of us seem prone to experience black times more intensely, and I guess I am one of those."

"Tell us what you mean by 'black times' and 'black thoughts,'" one of the participants asks. "I can never imagine someone like you thinking in black. You seem so willing to do such good things for people, I would expect that you would feel really good about yourself and your work most of the time."

"Well, I guess what we really need to talk about are all the times we experience the darker side of life. I have thought a lot about this since my days in Kalawao. I am a person who makes schedules and organizes things to be done, so I thought about all the ways life was hard for me and have put them into categories. Maybe Mother Teresa can add her own thoughts to these.

"For me, things fell into three boxes: the things that just happen as part of life, the ways we think our own thoughts and the ways other people treat us and others. All of these experiences can be helpful or can hurt. So much depends on how we react to them when they happen.

"In the first place, there are many things in life that are not the way we would like them. The leprosy I saw in so many people, their suffering and struggles, and my own leprosy come to mind. There were little children with leprosy, and many whose parents died with it, leaving them orphaned. We might try to find some reason why illness happens and may come up with all kinds of reasons, but look at the children. They surely did not bring it on themselves. So I do not believe God punishes us with bad things. I think they are just part of life, part of this imperfect world. Storms and floods and fires and hurricanes are part of it too. Death is part of life. Everything that lives has to die, whether we like it or not. We get old, we get sick, we weaken. We die. That's just the way things are."

"And that is what we must be willing to walk right into," Mother Teresa adds. "That is where we find the most needs of our sisters and brothers, and that is where we most especially find God. Often it is the dark places that challenge us. *For example, I think God is telling us something with AIDS, giving us an opportunity to show our love.*[4]

"Sometimes the darkness is there when we are trying to find our way. It is part of the journey, the struggle. Just because we choose to follow what God asks of us we should not expect it to be easy. I remember how when I had left the Loreto convent in Calcutta and was looking for a place to shelter the most needy, *I walked and walked*

*till I was exhausted. My hands and legs trembled with fatigue.
I finally understood how soul and body suffer among the poor
when they have to look for shelter, food and medicine. I can't
forget how easy everything was in the convent. This was a
temptation."*[5]

"I guess we can expect hard times in any situation,
even when we're trying to do good," one of the nurses
offers. "I heard another nurse one day say she felt like
every patient in the hospital rooms had an invisible
fishing line and hook that would catch her every time she
walked past their rooms. Needs were never totally met.
Sometimes she felt like she wanted to scream."

Father Damien joins in again, "That's what I mean by
my second group—how our own thoughts can create
blackness for us. It's true that things can be tough, that
we can find ourselves in the midst of awful things.
Mother Teresa and I and many of you have been in the
middle of places most people never want to go. Leprosy
and AIDS and cancer have not an iota of pleasantness
about them. Suffering people who are in pain or are
dying can tear the heart out of us. Our own weaknesses
and suffering can be miserable and lay us low. But all the
time, we have choices. We may not be able to change the
picture, but we can change how we look at it.

"My leprosy is an example. I vacillated in many
directions about it. I wanted to spend lots more time
caring for the others and could not believe my days
would be cut short. I fought the disease. I tried treatments
that were just experimental. Sometimes I felt despairing
and melancholic. Then I began to think about the leprosy
as my shortened road to heaven."

Mother Teresa adds, "Just because we are working
hard to follow God's way for us doesn't mean we won't
struggle with our own thoughts. I wrote in my diary
once, at a particularly difficult time, *I get the impression*

that I am living through a shipwreck in an ocean of sorrow and despair.[6] There have been other times when *I feel like an empty vessel, a limp rag. I feel so alone, so miserable.*[7] Don't any of you think we don't struggle with our own thoughts, just like you. Thoughts are important. What we let ourselves think has a lot to say about how we feel and what we do. And we're the ones who can change our thoughts. We're the only ones who can."

"I'm not sure, but maybe the third group is the hardest. But then, maybe dark times are all just hard and we don't need to compare them," Father Damien comes in again. He looks just a bit less depressed as he is able to talk about his hard times—a point important to remember.

"We can each be the source of all kinds of trouble for each other," he begins. "I was not an easy person to deal with. I dove in and had my own ideas about how my lepers should be treated, and about how I wanted to be treated. I was willing to give everything I had to make life better for them.

"People in authority did not always agree with me. My own superiors found me a problem. But the Board of Health did make me temporary superintendent of the operation till they found someone to do it. So they must have thought I did fairly well. They even wanted to pay me a salary for doing it, and I told them that *if I took their money my own mother would not recognize me as her child*![8] So I guess I was the source of trouble for some of them, though I never meant to be.

"Some of the other clergymen seemed angry about me and my work. A terrible letter was sent by one of them to a friend of his and wound up in the newspaper, calling me a 'coarse, dirty man, headstrong and bigoted.' He also accused me of 'relations with women,' and that my leprosy should be attributed to my 'vices and carelessness.'[9] When I received a decoration as Knight

Commander of the Royal Order of Kalakaua after the
Princess Regent Liliuokalani made a visit to the
settlement, many people were pleased but others were
again quite upset about it. One of the newspapers wrote,
'The prejudice, the spite and the mean spirit of certain
cliques' rose again after my award.[10] Of course, I only
wore the decoration on the day they gave it to me. When
someone expressed astonishment at not seeing it
displayed I told him *it would humiliate my old patched
cassock.*[11]

"The hardest experience for me came from my own
religious superiors. I must have rubbed them the wrong
way. Over the years, they did send a couple of priests to
share the work with me, but the priests never stayed. I
was so lonely and desperately wanted another priest to
be able to confess regularly. But about half of my time
there I was alone. They thought I received too much
attention in the press and from others who sent things for
my lepers from around the world. But I never asked for
that attention. Sometimes they said things to me that were
very painful for me. Because I did not receive much help
from them I tried to do the best I could by myself, but I
was told to be patient, that 'as soon as you are helpless,
you will have someone.' I also was told to 'make a
meditation on humility' before I wrote to my superiors."[12]

As a matter of record, Damien experienced painful
interaction with his immediate superiors. "If Damien had
the delusion of being unworthy of heaven, it was perhaps
because his superiors were leading him to believe it of
himself." They "continued to show a steady hostility
toward Damien, unchanged throughout 1887 and into
1888," the year before his death. They "continued to
blame him for what the world made of his heroism."
They accused him of "haughtiness." "They were as much
as putting him on trial, jeering at him, spitting in his face.

In imitation of Christ, he would try to suffer anything; but endurance was hard—harder, he said, than the bearing of his leprosy—when his superiors might well have seemed to him to be acting in imitation of Pilate."[13]

Damien looks quietly for a minute at the group around him. "Some of what they said about me was true. I was headstrong and determined to do what I thought my lepers needed. I was not as educated as I could have been, and so I was crude and my hands were dirty and callused from my work at times. Sometimes I overstepped my bounds. I had to pray hard and work hard to be what I should be and sometimes I did not get there."

A somber and quiet mood hangs heavily in the room. Dark clouds continue to make the world feel smaller. Many in the room are lost in their own thoughts of ineptness and inadequacy, in their own memories of suffering or in their present distress. And yet the two simple figures before them, he in his black tattered cassock and she in her simple white sari, bring them strength. No one is exempt from suffering. Not even those who laid their lives down for their brothers and sisters in need. If they could do it, if they could stay focused on what mattered, if they could make their way through the black times—and such intense black times as Damien described—so could we.

For Reflection

- *Spend fifteen or twenty minutes reflecting on the "dark" aspects of the natural world and how they affect your life. In what ways could you be the source of "black times" for others?*

- *What are your "black thoughts" about? Do they follow a common pattern?*

- *What are the painful experiences you meet as you live the life you believe God asks of you?*

- *How do you cope with your difficulties? What brings you strength during those times? How do you find God in your dark times?*

Closing Prayer

Hard as we try, O God, we cannot rid our lives of
   dark times.
And, much as we would prefer only the light times,
That is simply not the way you have made things
   here.
If that is the way things are,
If you are there in the dark as well as in the light,
May we walk into the dark without fear.

You said that those "who walked in darkness have
   seen a great light."[14]
May we count on that.
May we know that our darkness will be illuminated
   with your love and light.

Notes

[1] Daws, p. 48.
[2] Daws, p. 49.
[3] Isaiah 45:7.
[4] Lucinda Vardey, *Mother Teresa: A Simple Path* (New York: Ballantine, 1995), p. 87.
[5] Gjergji, p. 56.
[6] Gjergji, p. 55.
[7] Serrou, pp. 70-71.
[8] Daws, p. 92.

[9] Daws, p. 12.
[10] Englebert, p. 157.
[11] Englebert, p. 156.
[12] Daws, p. 185.
[13] Daws, pp. 185-186.
[14] Isaiah 9:1.

DAY SIX
Nourishment for the Journey

Coming Together in the Spirit

Many years ago I read the report of an interview with Dr. Victor Frankl, the Austrian psychiatrist, who had survived several years in concentration camps during the forties. In the course of questioning, the interviewer asked Dr. Frankl what it was that had sustained him during those horrifying, catastrophic times. The doctor slowly pondered the significance of the question, eager to respond in an honest, clear manner. His response when it came, went something like this: "I had a powerful source of support, a strong incentive to keep living, and living as well as I could. When things threatened to overwhelm me, I conjured up the image of my dear wife. I saw her in my mind waiting for me, sitting in the coziness of our favorite parlor, the warm glow of candlelight all around her. I held the thought of her for as long as I could and with it all the hope that it conjured up. Through the evening as the day darkened all around us I kept in my mind the light that the whole picture had become. That's what warmed and sustained me through my ordeal."

Defining Our Thematic Context

The dancer who pirouettes at a fantastic speed that dazzles the eye focuses on a point outside herself to maintain her balance. A person setting out on a strenuous course of study may keep in mind the value of what he hopes to achieve and what it will enable him to do with his life. That focus will keep him constant when times get rough and he feels inclined to give up. The parents who set out to raise their children to be strong, self-sufficient, healthy adults may find their nourishment from friends with similar values, from their faith in God and from their trust and love for each other.

Damien and Teresa knew clearly where their source of nourishment and energy lay. They shared that source. Both were like dancers who had a focus that fed, nourished and inspired them. Through all the rigors of their chosen lives, through many hardships and harsh criticisms, neither of them wavered. Today they encourage us to be sure we are solidly grounded ourselves. They know that we will not get very far without a focus that will never leave us, that is solidly trustworthy and dependable. They tell us what they fed on that supported and comforted them, in hopes that we will each develop an awareness of our own source of nourishment. They strongly push us to feed deeply on the "food" available in God's banquet all around us.

Opening Prayer

O God, who provides a banquet for us
Beyond our wildest imagining,
More food than we ever need for our journeys,
Help us to dive in with gusto.

Whatever our ways of spending ourselves in this
world,
We need to be replenished.
We cannot do it without you.

Remind us that this banquet is always available,
Even when we turn to less substantial food that does
not nourish.
You supply food for our souls in so many forms:
In those who love us,
In all your creation,
Even in our hard times, and in those who do not love
us, and in darkness.
You give us yourself.

Let us hold on to our belief that we can always count
on you,
In good times and in harsh times.
You surround us with opportunities to nourish our
minds, hearts and souls.

Retreat Session Six

Only two more days for us to be together, and our
group is eager to absorb as much wisdom as we can from
our mentors. We fill our meeting room early, not wanting
to miss out on anything that might be said. Teresa and
Damien come in together, he moving with some effort,
but a brighter look on his face. Gone is the dark mood of
the day before. They smile in delight when they see us
there waiting for them, and settle into their chairs.

"Father Damien and I have been talking about how
we want to organize today's program," Mother Teresa
said, "and we want it to be a real give-and-take among all

of us. We know none of you would be here if you did not already have a source of support that has helped you get to this day. Some of you may be feeling low, but that's all right. All the more reason for us to share with each other. One of the closest and best ways God supports us is through those around us. We just need to have ears to hear and eyes to recognize God's presence here. And we need to be open to receive it. We'll share our own ideas, the things that sustained us, but we also want you to learn from each other."

"Well, I can tell you one thing I have picked up from both of you," one of the nurses says. "God is a real person to you. I have believed in God all my life, but I have to say that God is pretty distant and not very involved with me and my daily life. You both sound like God is somebody you know. I wish I could be that close."

"That's what prayer does for me," Mother Teresa answers. "And that's what my mother taught me as a little girl. I find that when I keep talking to God, when I keep looking for him because I know God is everywhere and in all the people I meet, pretty soon he becomes more and more real. He *is* real! I am not doing anything extraordinary, I am just connecting to him in everything I do. *Prayer begets faith, faith begets love, and love begets service on behalf of the poor.*"[1]

Both Teresa and Damien came from traditional Christian homes in which their mothers saw to it that the family lived in close accord with the Catholic Church. Both engaged in family prayer and good works, assisting those in need in their neighborhoods. They illustrate well the significance of early seeds of faith, planted and watered within an environment of belief and practice. In their youth they were somewhat protected from the questioning of religious beliefs and values going on in the world at large.

Throughout their lives, Damien and Teresa stayed close to those early lessons. Neither seemed to question what they were taught and believed, but instead practiced it scrupulously, unaffected by differing beliefs.

> Mother Teresa has her principles, and as noted before, she has learned these principles at her mother's knee. It is difficult to reproach her for them, even if she irritates certain people with her insistent prayers to the Sacred Heart and the Virgin. In the name of principles stemming from her childhood, she proves to be intransigent.[2]

Does that mean her beliefs, and Damien's beliefs so like hers, are the only way we can journey toward God? Can we find inspiration in their ways and yet be aware of our own abilities to discover how God is at work in each of us? Can we accept the differences, and the responsibility to follow God's lead in our own unique lives?

"I do not think I can pray quite like you do," an ailing participant says. "I do not find much help in saying some of the prayers I learned as a little girl. They feel too formal to me. I have to talk to God—actually to Jesus most of the time—in *my* words. I can imagine him sitting down with me like a friend would, and just being there. Sometimes that's what helps me fall asleep when I am upset or in pain, I know he would say he would stay there and not leave while I rest. Then I can relax."

"I pray best outside, especially in the trees in the mountains," another participant adds, "or in my back yard."

"I go to Mass every morning," says another, "and for me that's a great way to start the day. I feel like it just helps me put everything in perspective. Once I have been there, I can handle whatever the day brings."

One of the nurses says, "When I go to work, I say to God, 'I want everything I do today to be a prayer—

whether I'm passing out medicines or changing a dressing, or talking to a doctor, or bringing a lunch tray to a patient—I want it all to be done in your name. Please let me be the channel through which you do all these things and love all these people.'"

"The important thing," Father Damien breaks in, "is that we pray. Because prayer is being in contact with God. We do not do it for God; we do it for ourselves, to keep us aware of and connected to God's presence. We each need to figure out our own way to do this. Just like we treat one person differently than another, we have to figure out and maintain the unique relationship we have with God."

"Hearing one of you talk about attending Mass, I want to say something that I believe is a powerful source of nourishment," Mother Teresa interjects. *"If we make the Eucharist the central focus of our lives, if we feed our lives with the Eucharist, we will not find it difficult to discover Christ, to love him, and to serve him in the poor.*[3] And do not forget all the prayers to Mary we can say. She is a great source of support for us."

"As a mother myself," one participant notes, "I turn to her all the time. She has been a real model and inspiration for me in caring for my own children. She did not have it very easy in her life either."

Father Damien nods in agreement and opens another area to consider. "Let's move on from here, and look at how our work itself nourishes us. Mother Teresa and I were challenged by God to care for his people in need. Just like she said before, it's through our faith that love and service come about. Then, if we follow those inspirations, we will be sustained by the very service we give.

"Our faith did not keep us tied to the things of our youth, it eventually challenged us to live in some rather radical ways. Though we believed in authority, we both

took it upon ourselves to confront authority and follow
the ways we believed God was leading us. She left her
religious community—a place where she was comfortable
and able to do good work—to put herself into a risky,
insecure situation. I cannot believe everyone was pleased
about her decision! I went over the head of my immediate
superior and wrote to the Father General—a brash and
unheard of move on the part of a young seminarian—at a
time in my life when I felt called to the missions in place
of my ailing brother. Neither of us just sat back and
waited for someone else to tell us what God wanted of us.
From somewhere inside we found an ability to trust in
ourselves.

"If we are willing to trust God's presence within and
connect with that presence, we will be nourished and
given the strength for whatever he asks. The work itself
will be a source of food for us. I know we both have
found that to be true. Many times with my lepers, even in
terrible conditions, I found a warmth and joy as I cared
for them."

"I had that experience one day with a young girl from
outside India who came to join us," Mother Teresa says.
*"We have a rule that the very next day new arrivals must go to
the Home for the Dying. So I told this girl: 'You saw Father
during Holy Mass, with what love and care he touched Jesus in
the Host. Do the same when you go to the Home for the Dying,
because it is the same Jesus you will find there in the broken
bodies of our poor.' And they went. After three hours the
newcomer came back and said to me with a big smile—I have
never seen a smile quite like that—'Mother, I have been
touching the body of Christ for three hours.' And I said to her:
'How—what did you do?' She replied: 'When we arrived there,
they brought a man who had fallen into a drain, and been there
for some time. He was covered with wounds and dirt and
maggots, and I cleaned him and I knew I was touching the*

body of Christ.'"[4]

As the time comes to a close, there follows a lively give-and-take of personal experiences of support. Father Damien tells of the "Personal Rule" he drew up for himself so he could organize and remember everything he wanted to include in his daily routine. He also describes how important people were to him, how much he loved company and how lonely he felt without a priest companion. He found great support and nourishment from people and maintained a regular letter-writing relationship with his brother.

"I love to read," one participant says, "I'm so busy so much of the time that some of my most important times are when I can sit quietly and read good things. I learned about meditative reading, and that helps, but so do lots of other spiritual and psychological books. What I read helps me learn about myself and other people, and gives me lots of good things to think about."

"And meditation...," says another. "I could not live peacefully for long without meditation."

"You can see," Mother Teresa brings the morning to a close, "that we each need to find what nourishes us. We each might make a plan for what is helpful and build it into our everyday lives. We get into trouble, not by doing a lot, but when we do not build in opportunities to replenish ourselves as we go along. God gives us so many sources of nourishment. Be sure you find what best enables you to be what you are called to be."

For Reflection

- *What nourishes and sustains you in your daily life?*

- *How do you build opportunities for self-nourishment into each day?*

- *How does your work sustain and nourish you?*

- *Consider drawing up a "personal rule" of sorts to remind yourself of activities you want to incorporate on a daily basis.*

- *What new ideas come to you from Damien and Teresa that you could make your own?*

Closing Prayer

O God, in whatever ways we choose to nurture
    ourselves,
May you always be the source of that nourishment.

Mother Teresa said, *"The hardest thing in life is to
    maintain one's balance."*[5]
Keep us in balance.

May what we empty out in your name,
what we give to others,
what we suffer in our own lives,
always be filled up by you.
You are the only source of lasting nourishment.

Notes

[1] Mother Teresa, *In My Own Words* (Ligouri, Mo.: Ligouri Publications, 1996), p. 7.

[2] Serrou, p. 75.

[3] Mother Teresa, p. 97.

[4] Serrou, pp. 50-51.

[5] Gjergji, p. 53.

DAY SEVEN
Here I Am, Lord

Coming Together in the Spirit

In *Soul Food: Stories to Nourish the Spirit and the Heart*, there is this thought-provoking tale:

> There's a monk who will never give you advice, but only a question. I was told his questions could be very helpful. I sought him out. "I am a parish priest," I said. "I'm here on retreat. Could you give me a question?"
>
> "Ah, yes," he answered. "My question is, 'What do they need?'"
>
> I came away disappointed. I spent a few hours with the question, writing out answers, but finally I went back to him.
>
> "Excuse me. Perhaps I didn't make myself clear. Your question has been helpful, but I wasn't so much interested in thinking about my apostolate during this retreat. Rather I wanted to think seriously about my own spiritual life. Could you give me a question for my own spiritual life?"
>
> "Ah, I see. Then my question is, 'What do they *really* need?'"[1]

Defining Our Thematic Context

Everything works together. Everything is interconnected—giving and receiving from everything else in an endless process. When we see clearly—the way God sees—we find God everywhere. When we find God everywhere, we find ourselves compelled to let go of all that is unimportant and reach out to serve God. Even though darkness and difficulty may divert us from our course, we are compelled to serve God in some way. This is the message Mother Teresa and Father Damien have brought us during this retreat.

Life may not ask us to go to India or Hawaii, but Calcutta and Molokai are all around us. Our own spirituality is tied up with how we respond to the world in which we live—the poor and the lepers certainly, as well as all who are hungry or needy, even in our own homes. We all are called upon to serve each other. We need each other for our own wholeness and salvation. "Come, you that are blessed by my Father, inherit the kingdom prepared for you from the foundation of the world; for I was hungry..."[2]

On this last day with our mentors they challenge all of us—not just those who have chosen care-giving as a profession—to care for each other. The cost will be high if we agree. It will be even higher if we refuse.

Opening Prayer

O God, who reaches out with the gift of life to
   each of us,
Who supports and sustains us in our lives,
Help us to share that gift with each other.
Help us to see that all life is giving and receiving,

And that not one of us has any more right to it than
   any other.

When we reach out with love and care to each other,
In the very giving of ourselves,
We unite with you who are yourself the gift of life.
May we and those for whom we care
Grow in that union with you.

RETREAT SESSION SEVEN

"One of the big mistakes we make in this world is
when we think only some of us are called to care for
others," Father Damien begins. "We recognize those who
have chosen to spend their lives in one of the helping
professions, and then think we can delegate all of our
responsibility to them. The truth is twofold: that they are
fortunate to have work that offers great blessings in all
directions; and, though we may not be professional caregivers, we are all in God's world together and have a
responsibility to care for each other."

"There's never enough time to do all that needs to be
done," Mother Teresa joins in, "and our time here with
you is almost over. If each of us does not have a sense of
our responsibility for each other and how it grows out of
what we've said, we want today to bring all of it together
and see how we can make sense of it in our own
individual lives. So let's spend today talking about how
we give care to those in need."

Damien continues, "This caring for others is the
natural result of all we have been considering this week.
If we make the effort to see the world and everything in it
God's way, we will begin to let go of everything—inside

and out—that prevents us from seeing clearly. We will also be able to see the hunger and need in others when we're not blinded by so many unimportant things in our own lives. Then reaching out to those who need our love and care will feel like the natural thing to do."

"It is going to cost us something though, so we have to work and pray not to be overwhelmed by hard times, dark times. There is nothing easy about all this. But if we have a source of nourishment we can count on, and if we find blessings from what we're doing, we will be able to hold to the task and find that it brings blessing to us along with blessing the other."

"Before we go on," a woman in the group says, "I want to tell you about my experience. I was one of those people who never had any interest in taking care of anyone else. I would get as far away from sick people as I could. My motto was 'Let somebody else do it, somebody who feels noble and good about cleaning up after the sick.' And then the bottom dropped out. We had a baby that we never expected to be able to have when we were older, and she was born with all kinds of problems. At first, I did my usual thing and we put her in a hospital or someplace. I just could not accept her and did not want to have anything to do with her.

"But she kept nagging at my thoughts until I finally couldn't take it anymore. We brought her home when she was five months old, and I have cared for her since. At first it was hard. And even though she grew, the biggest change was in me. I do not see her as deformed and ugly anymore—she's precious to me. It feels like when I opened up to her and began to love her, she and I both became different people. She is an enormous gift to me now, even though she's hard to care for. And, when I started seeing the gift and beauty in her, other people with problems and handicaps started looking different to me, too. It's hard to explain what happened."

"I think you have just described the transforming power of love," Mother Teresa says. "When we see with eyes of love, we have a different vision. We begin looking with God's eyes."

Father Damien wants to add his own thoughts and begins speaking about his lepers. "I chose to be there. And yet, at first it was hard. The deformities, the missing fingers and ears and toes, the open sores and the maggots, and the smell. I felt sick so many times. And then gradually my experience changed. As I began to know the lepers and see them more often, my own experience was transformed, too. Many of them became beautiful people to me. But it took being able to change my way of looking. My faith and desire to do good work took me there, but my change of seeing and my love grew out of my willingness to be with the people."

"Let's talk more about how we go about our care," Mother Teresa says. "I think a lot of people think you have to do extraordinary things. Sometimes that's true. But most of the time what we do for each other is really ordinary. I want to talk about some of those ordinary things that I think are necessary and important in what we do.

"*Let there be kindness in your face, in your eyes, in your smile, in the warmth of your greeting. For children, for the poor, for all those who suffer, and are alone, always have a cheerful smile. Don't only give your care, but give your heart as well.... When you attend to the wounds and bruises of the poor, never forget that they are Christ's wounds.*[3]

"There are other thoughts I share with those who come to work with me. *Let no one ever come to you without leaving better and happier. Be the living expression of God's kindness, kindness in your face, kindness in your eyes, kindness in your smile. Don't look for spectacular actions. What is*

*important is the gift of yourselves. It is the degree of love that
you invest in each of your deeds. Thoughtfulness is the
beginning of great sanctity. Our vocation, to be beautiful, must
be full of thought for others."*[4]

"I think it's important to talk about how hard it is
sometimes," Father Damien adds. "When we talk about
the blessing of caring for those in need, I know I had a
pretty unreal idea that it would all be easy since I was
doing it for God. There were times, even with the best of
intentions, that I almost couldn't do it. *From morning to
night, I would be amidst heartbreaking physical and moral
misery. Still, I'd try to appear always gay, so as to raise the
courage of my patients."*[5]

"Nobody yet has said anything about caring for
yourself, when you are the one who is suffering." The
voice comes from the woman with cancer who struggled
with feelings of self-worth.

"I think all the same things apply," a nurse
volunteers. "I think if we really treated ourselves like
each of you has suggested we treat other people, we
wouldn't suffer nearly as much as we do. I do think some
of our suffering comes from how we talk to ourselves
about what's happening in us."

"I know what you mean," the woman replies.
"Sometimes I wake up in a fairly peaceful place, and by
the time I finish telling myself how awful life is, and what
a terrible person I must be to have had this happen to me,
and how life is never going to be the same, and how
afraid I am to die, there's no smile, no 'leaving me better'
than I was before I started beating up on myself. There's
no love for myself in all of that. Then I keep waiting for
somebody else, maybe God, to come and heal me, to
make everything better."

"The same thing can happen when you're the care-
giver," another nurse offers. "I can sometimes find such

joy in what I'm able to do and be for sick people, and I can feel so blessed and see all the gifts coming to me. Other times I'm my own worst enemy. Somebody doesn't follow my directions, or keeps asking me for help when I have a million things to do, or somehow rubs me the wrong way and I'm off on a tear in my own mind about how hard the work is, how ungrateful people are, how nobody cares how I feel. Maybe this is a common human trait, but somehow I'd like to learn how to handle it better."

A social worker speaks up for the first time. "We need to be aware of our expectations. When we set up a grandiose plan that we're going to take care of all things for all people and only receive gratitude, and that we're going to breeze through it with nothing but good feelings, we're dooming ourselves to failure. That's looking for perfection. Even Jesus didn't find everyone open and receptive and grateful for what he offered. I think even our 'failures' and our hard times offer us something."

"What do you mean?" Mother Teresa listens intently.

"Well, I read about a care-giver who was exhausting herself in caring for others. One day, one of those people wasn't very pleasant or cooperative, but challenged the care-giver to, in essence, 'cure me.' The care-giver said she felt a blaze of anger sweep over her and wanted to explode at the insolent demand. And then she stopped, and said to herself, 'I'm going to sit here till I figure out what the gift is in what this man just said to me.' It changed the course of her work. She could see later that the very challenge that so angered and upset her was just what she needed to change her own attitude about what she was doing. She said she had to recognize that she wasn't the one who cures, but rather only one person who is willing to be with people in their suffering and by being there help them to see their own way to the peace and healing God makes available within them."

Mother Teresa smiles. "I've always said that *I feel like a pencil in God's hand*, that it is he who had done everything. It has all been his work.[6] You know, the pencil provides God with what he needs to do his work here. A pencil without that hand to guide it can't do much."

"We just have to remember that the hand of God is always holding us," Father Damien adds, "even when we feel worn down to a little stub, God can still write."

Outside the windows the sun has returned, and with it a sky of deep blue. Birds know the rainstorm brought treasures out of the ground for them and are hopping, strutting and pecking in their search. We sit in quiet reflection.

Father Damien seems to be musing aloud, from deep within his own reverie, "You know, I'm thinking that healing and cure come in all kinds of ways, and that neither Mother Teresa nor I were asked by God to cure the physical ravages of leprosy or the diseases that grow from poverty. We would have been happy to be able to do that, don't get me wrong.

"What we actually did, the both of us, is just what you said," he nods toward the social worker who had spoken. "We were both there with our own presence and love and caring, to be with people in their suffering and need. We also gave God a place through our physical presence to love and care for and be with the poor and suffering, who have always been precious in his sight. I hope through our love for them, and our respect for their dignity, that they were able to find within themselves, from the God within, whatever healing of spirit or soul they needed. That's basically what Jesus did most of the time he was on earth.

"That's what every one of us can do. That's what you came to do, little mother, when you cared for your child who came packaged in a way that hid the God within. Something kept you looking—perhaps the God in you. And that's what you're searching for," he nods toward the frail woman in the wheelchair, "though you are having a hard time finding God in your own dark places. Others may see him in you, but you seem to still be struggling with your darkness which holds the key to healing of some kind for you.

"That's an important lesson for all of us—to remember that God is just as present in darkness as in light. I had a hard time with that, too," he says to the woman in the wheelchair. "One of the biggest costs to us in coming to wholeness, and also in our caring for others, is having to let go of our old ways of believing or of doing things. It's hard to let go."

Mother Teresa smiles at Father Damien, and then extends her brilliant smile to the group. "So here we've come to the end of our time together, searchers all," she says quietly. "How good it's been for us to be together. May we go knowing we have God's blessing."

For Reflection

- *What are the gifts you have to offer to people in need? What do you think are your special gifts?*

- *What are the ways you might be more loving and respectful of yourself?*

- *In what ways do you already reach out in caring to others—people, animals, the world?*

- *In what ways might you be setting up expectations of perfection in your care-giving, or of others for whom you may care?*

■ *Where do you find the differences between God's thoughts and your thoughts?*

Closing Prayer

O God, thank you for the gift of this time with Teresa
  and Damien.
Thank you for the examples of their lives,
for the ways they have shown us how to see
  differently.
Most especially, we want to thank you for their
  qualities and inspiration,
For their singleness of purpose,
For their commitment to your broken people,
For their willingness to spend their lives so lavishly
  for you,
For their steadfastness when times were harsh and
  dark,
For their never counting the cost, for never turning
  back,
For their courage in taking your path in a world that
  leads elsewhere,
For all the ways love shines from their lives.

May all these qualities find a home in us.
May we nurture them and see them bear much fruit
In our own growth and our care and love for others.

Notes

[1] Father Theophane, quoted in Jack Kornfield and Christina
  Feldman, eds. *Soul Food: Stories to Nourish the Spirit and the Heart*
  (San Francisco: HarperSanFrancisco, 1996), pp. 124-125.

[2] Matthew 25:34-35.

[3] Serrou, p. 58.
[4] Serrou, pp. 76-78.
[5] Daws, p. 86.
[6] Serrou, p. 87.

Going Forth to Live the Theme

Some years back in my hospital counseling, I was asked to see a patient with an incurable cancer. He was an older, brilliant man, a professor of hard science, a man who wasn't ready to die. I was young in the profession, but already blessed by many experiences with people moving toward death. I approached his room anticipating the unique and individual sadness and struggle, as well as the potential for closeness and warmth that tended to bless such a time. What I found was my delayed baptism of blood.

"What do you think you are going to do?" he as much as sneered as I walked into the room. "I don't want any of your psychological stuff tried on me!" he shouted. That was the beginning of a difficult, challenging relationship that called forth honesty, understanding, empathy and caring in ways I'd never quite experienced before. He really did want me there. But he wanted no games. It was one of the hardest experiences I'd ever had. But he helped me hone my attention and question my efforts in ways no one had ever done. He was a gift—but not an easy gift to receive.

Spending a week with Damien and Teresa might be similar to walking into such a situation. They hit us between the eyes with the challenge of their lives. Now it's time to ask ourselves what it all meant to us. What did we find in who they were and what they said that we could make our own? To what degree do we wish to follow them? Why?

Maybe we can also examine how we disagree with them and their ways. What didn't we like about them? What would be our conflicts if we sat down and talked with them? Just like the patient I saw with cancer, the patient who made life difficult for me in his exacting expectations of honesty and care, their ways can carry great challenge.

Whatever we find in the evaluation of our time together, these are people—Teresa and Damien—we can never forget. Not many will choose to follow the rigors of their lives, though some will. Perhaps their greatest gift to us is not to expect us to follow them exactly in their vocations, but to listen for the ways God calls each of us in our own lives. Each of us can be challenged by their originality—their willingness to stretch themselves, to go places that few had ever gone—both in the external world and into their own beings. They were willing to hear and to follow the beat of their own drummers.

And finally, they challenge us by their ability to find God in all his distressing disguises. If we do only that, this week will have brought us reward.

Deepening Your Acquaintance

Books by and about Mother Teresa

Chawla, Navin. *Mother Teresa: The Authorized Biography*. Rockport, Mass: Element, 1998.

Gjergji, Lush. *Mother Teresa: Her Life, Her Works*. Hyde Park, N.Y.: New City Press, 1991.

Mother Teresa. *In My Own Words*. Compiled by Jose Luis Gonzalez-Balado. Liguori, Mo.: Liguori Publications, 1996.

___. *A Simple Path*. Compiled by Lucinda Vardey. New York: Ballantine Books, 1995.

Muggeridge, Malcolm. *Something Beautiful for God: Mother Teresa of Calcutta*. New York: Harper & Row, 1971.

Serrou, Robert. *Teresa of Calcutta: A Pictorial Biography*. New York: McGraw-Hill, 1980.

Books about Father Damien

Englebert, Omer. *Damien: Hero of Molokai*. Boston: St. Paul Books and Media, 1994.

Farrow, John. *Damien the Leper*. New York: Image/Doubleday, 1954.

Daws, Gavan. *Holy Man: Father Damien of Molokai*. New York: Harper & Row, 1973.

Videos

Mother Teresa. Available from Videos With Values.

Mother Teresa: A Life of Devotion. Available from Ignatius Press.